defining eclipse

defining eclipse

Vocabulary Workbook for Unlocking the *SAT, ACT®, GED®, and SSAT®

Brian Leaf, M.A.

WILEY

Wiley Publishing, Inc.

Library of Congress Cataloging-in-Publication Data:
Leaf, Brian.
  Defining eclipse: vocabulary workbook for unlocking the SAT, ACT, GED, and SSAT / by Brian Leaf.
    p. cm.
  ISBN 978-0-470-59696-8(pbk)
  ISBN: 978-0-470-63048-8(ebk)
  1. Vocabulary tests--Study guides. 2. Vocabulary--Study and teaching (Secondary). I. Title.
  PE1449.L31 2010
  428.1'076--dc21
                    2010007221

Printed in the United States of America

10 9 8 7 6 5 4 3 2 1

Book production by Wiley Publishing, Inc., Composition Services

Acknowledgments ·

Thanks to Stephenie Meyer for her storytelling and her terrific vocabulary. Thanks to my agent, Linda Roghaar, and my fantastic editors at Wiley, Greg Tubach and Carol Pogoni. Thanks to Amy Sell, Malati Chavali, and Adrienne Fontaine at Wiley for getting the word out. Thanks to Heidi and Maddy Bennett for their *Twilight* expertise. Thanks to Pam Weber-Leaf for great editing tips, Zach Nelson for sage marketing advice, Ian Curtis for assiduous proofreading, Manny and Susan Leaf for everything, and of course, thanks most of all to Gwen, Noah, and Benjamin for love, support, and inspiration. This book is dedicated in loving memory of Gary Willick (we all miss you, "Pop").

Table of Contents

About the Author

Brian Leaf, M.A., is the author of *Defining Twilight, Defining New Moon,* and the four-book SAT and ACT test-prep series *McGraw-Hill's Top 50 Skills for a Top Score*. He is Director of the New Leaf Learning Center in Massachusetts, and has provided SAT, ACT, GED, SSAT, and GRE preparation to thousands of students throughout the United States. Brian also works with the Georgetown University Office of Undergraduate Admissions as an alumni interviewer, and is a certified yoga instructor and avid meditator. For more information, visit his Web site at www.brianleaf.com.

How to Use This Book

This workbook contains 40 groups of vocabulary words selected from *Eclipse*. Many of these words will show up on your SAT, ACT, GED, or SSAT. Beginning at Group 1, refer to the *Eclipse* page where each vocabulary word appears. Read the word in context and come up with a definition. Then check your definitions against those provided in this workbook and make corrections. I'll also show you synonyms, word parts, and memorization tools. Read these over a few times, and then complete the drills. Do that for all 40 groups. There's no easier or more fun way to learn 600 vocabulary words! By the end of this book, your vocabulary will be larger, your test scores will be higher, and you'll be an *Eclipse* scholar!

Group 1
Subterfuge

Find each of the following words on the *Eclipse* page number provided. Based on the way each word is used in the book, guess at its definition.

1. **Subterfuge** (p. 1) might mean _____

_____

2. **In vain** (p. 1) might mean _____

_____

3. **Diverted** (p. 2) might mean _____

_____

4. **Ultimatum** (p. 3) might mean _____

_____

5. **Hemorrhage** (p. 4) might mean _____

_____

6. **Essence** (p. 5) might mean _____

_____

7. **Surly** (p. 6) might mean _____

_____

8. **Hokey** (p. 6) might mean _____

_____

Let's see how you did. Check your answers, write the exact definitions, and reread the sentence in *Eclipse* where each word appears. Then complete the drills on the next page.

1. **Subterfuge** (p. 1) means *trickery* or *deception*. This is a great word to break apart. The prefix *sub-* can mean *under,* as in the word *subterranean,* meaning *underground,* and *-fuge* means *escape,* as in *refuge* and *fugitive.* So *subterfuge* means *escape under (as in undercover), by trickery or deception.* Synonyms: artifice, chicanery, duplicity, guile.

2. **In vain** (p. 1) means *useless.* Synonym: futile.

3. **Diverted** (p. 2) means *distracted.* Of course you knew that, but I included this word to mention the high-level SAT and ACT word *diversion* that means *recreation* or *entertainment,* as in "The king was diverted by the court jester's diversions." Often reading-comprehension questions ask which meaning of a word is implied in a passage. You can always tell by the context, and in this case the hungry vampire is waiting for Edward to be distracted, not entertained!

4. **Ultimatum** (p. 3) means *final demand, usually given as a threat.* That makes sense since *ultim-* implies *final* or *end,* as in the word *ultimate.*

5. **Hemorrhage** (p. 4) means *burst of blood,* and in fact *hemo-* implies *blood* as in *hemoglobin* (a component of blood) and *hemophiliac* (a person whose blood does not clot properly).

6. **Essence** (p. 5) means *fundamental nature.* Synonyms: crux, quintessence.

7. **Surly** (p. 6) means *rude and unfriendly.* Synonyms: abrupt, brusque, cantankerous, churlish, curt.

8. **Hokey** (p. 6) means *corny, overused,* or *overly sentimental.* Standardized tests love the related words *banal* (overused and boring); and *cliché, hackneyed, platitudinous,* and *trite* which all mean *overused.* Don't you love that your SAT, ACT, GED, or SSAT score will go up from reading the *Twilight* saga!

Synonyms: Select the word or phrase whose meaning is closest to the word in capital letters.

1. SUBTERFUGE
   A. underground
   B. artifice
   C. blood burst
   D. quintessence
   E. crux

2. ULTIMATUM
   A. diversion
   B. chicanery
   C. duplicity
   D. final demand
   E. guile

3. SURLY
   A. churlish
   B. banal
   C. cliché
   D. hackneyed
   E. platitudinous

4. HOKEY
   A. deceptive
   B. futile
   C. in vain
   D. ultimate
   E. trite

Analogies: Select the answer choice that best completes the meaning of the sentence.

5. Spy is to subterfuge as
   A. doctor is to hemorrhage
   B. Voldemort is to essence
   C. magician is to diversion
   D. architect is to artifice
   E. Edward is to Bella's hemoglobin

6. Surly is to pleasant as
   A. abrupt is to brusque
   B. kind is to sweet
   C. cantankerous is to churlish
   D. curt is to friendly
   E. hokey is to trite

Sentence Completions: Choose the word that, when inserted in the sentence, *best* fits the meaning of the sentence as a whole.

7. The columnist was known for his trademark _____ and corny phrases.
   A. brusque
   B. ultimate
   C. hackneyed
   D. futile
   E. duplicitous

8. Hoping to capture the _____ of the matter in only three lines, Miguel wrote a haiku entitled "Quintessence."
   A. diversion
   B. crux
   C. hemorrhage
   D. churlishness
   E. chicanery

1. **B.** *Subterfuge* and *artifice* mean *deception. Crux* means *essence.* That's why the magical items that Voldemort uses to hide parts of his **soul** (his essence) are called horcruxes!

2. **D.** *Ultimatum* means *final demand.* Use the process of elimination—cross out all choices that are **definitely** wrong. *Diversion* means *distraction* or *entertainment;* and *chicanery, duplicity,* and *guile* mean *deception. Duplicity* is the title of the Julia Roberts and Clive Owen movie about two spies who try to **trick/deceive** corporations.

3. **A.** *Surly* and *churlish* mean *rude and unfriendly. Banal, cliché, hackneyed,* and *platitudinous* mean *overused.*

4. **E.** *Hokey* and *trite* mean *overused. Futile* and *in vain* mean *useless.*

5. **C.** Make a sentence with the two words. For example, "A spy might use subterfuge (deception)." Then, try your sentence for each pair of words in the answer choices.
   - A. A doctor might use a hemorrhage . . . no, she or he might stop a hemorrhage.
   - B. Voldemort might use essence . . . no, though he did use a hor**crux.**
   - (C.) A magician might use a diversion (distraction) . . . yes!
   - D. An architect might use artifice (tricks) . . . no, not necessarily.
   - E. Edward might use Bella's hemoglobin (blood) . . . No way, come on! Victoria is dying to "use" Bella's hemoglobin, but Edward, no way!

6. **D.** "Surly is the opposite of pleasant."
   - A. Abrupt is the opposite of brusque . . . no, they both mean *rude and unfriendly.*
   - B. Kind is the opposite of sweet . . . no.
   - C. Cantankerous is the opposite of churlish . . . no, they both mean *rude and unfriendly.*
   - (D.) Curt is the opposite of friendly . . . yes!
   - E. Hokey is the opposite of trite . . . no, they both mean *overused.*

7. **C.** Think of a word to fill the blank. Often you can borrow a word right out of the sentence.

   > "The columnist was known for his trademark *corny* and corny phrases."

   Use the process of elimination, crossing off answer choices that **definitely** do not work, and then see which answer choice fits best. *Hackneyed* means *corny* and is the best answer.

8. **B.** "Hoping to capture the *quintessence* of the matter in only three lines, Miguel wrote a haiku entitled 'Quintessence.'"

   When trying to come up with a word to fill the blank, always look for evidence in the sentence—"quintessence" tells you what you need. *Crux* and *quintessence* mean *essence.*

Group 2
Conditional Parole

Find each of the following words on the *Eclipse* page number provided.
Based on the way each word is used in the book, guess at its definition.

1. **Fiancée** (p. 6) might mean _____

_____

2. **Orchestrate** (p. 7) might mean _____

_____

3. **On the sly** (p. 7) might mean _____

_____

4. **Escalation** (p. 7) might mean _____

_____

5. **Stringent** (p. 7) might mean _____

_____

6. **Scathingly** (p. 9) might mean _____

_____

7. **Parole** (p. 10) might mean _____

_____

8. **Conditionally** (p. 11) might mean _____

_____

Let's see how you did. Check your answers, write the exact definitions, and reread the sentence in *Eclipse* where each word appears. Then complete the drills on the next page.

1. **Fiancée** (p. 6) means *woman engaged to be married.* Interestingly, a man about to be married is a *fiancé,* with only one, rather than two *e*'s at the end of the word. Synonym: betrothed.

2. **Orchestrate** (p. 7) means *plan or arrange the various parts of something to produce a certain result,* like conducting all the instruments in an **orchestra** to create a symphony.

3. **On the sly** (p. 7) means *secretly.* You see lots of great vocab words in the *Twilight* series for *secretly*—can you guess why? Some of the synonyms you see are *clandestinely, covertly, furtively,* and *surreptitiously.*

4. **Escalation** (p. 7) means *increase or bring things to the next level,* just like the **escalator** brings you to the **next level** in the mall. Synonyms: amplification, augmentation, exacerbation (increase and make worse).

5. **Stringent** (p. 7) means *strict.* Synonym: stern.

6. **Scathingly** (p. 9) means *with criticism and anger.* You can usually figure out the definition of a word from the *context* (the words and sentences around it). Charlie and Bella are talking about Jacob getting Bella grounded, and Charlie says that what Jacob did was "responsible," to which Bella responds **scathingly,** "rolling her eyes." You know that she is **critical and angry** because of the context. The SAT, ACT, GED, and SSAT do this also; they always define a word in the words and sentences around it.

7. **Parole** (p. 10) means *release with the promise of good behavior. Parole* actually comes from the French word for *word,* since *parole* is giving one's **word** (promising good behavior).

8. **Conditionally** (p. 11) means *with a condition or reservation.* Standardized tests love to test the word *conditional* and its synonyms, which are *mitigated, qualified,* and *tempered.*

Synonyms: Select the word or phrase whose meaning is closest to the word in capital letters.

1. ORCHESTRATE
   A . divert
   B . arrange
   C . amplify
   D . augment
   E . exacerbate

2. SLY
   A . scathing
   B . futile
   C . diverted
   D . essential
   E . furtive

3. STRINGENT
   A . hokey
   B . banal
   C . stern
   D . cliché
   E . trite

4. CONDITIONAL
   A . qualified
   B . escalated
   C . duplicitous
   D . ultimate
   E . surreptitious

Analogies: Select the answer choice that best completes the meaning of the sentence.

5. Covert is to furtive as
   A . ultimate is to conditional
   B . scathing is to quiet
   C . surly is to mitigated
   D . subterfuge is to trickery
   E . paroled is to stringent

6. Escalation is to augmentation as
   A . amplification is to exacerbation
   B . orchestration is to ultimatum
   C . artifice is to hemorrhage
   D . chicanery is to honesty
   E . diversion is to ruination

Sentence Completions: Choose the word that, when inserted in the sentence, *best* fits the meaning of the sentence as a whole.

7. John and his fiancée _____ their entire wedding; they chose the date, made the seating chart, selected the music, and planned the entire menu.
   A . orchestrated
   B . paroled
   C . exacerbated
   D . hemorrhaged
   E . diverted

8. Afraid that she would be denied parole from her grounding, Jessica held back any _____ remarks to her parents.
   A . hokey
   B . hackneyed
   C . conditional
   D . scathing
   E . mitigated

1. **B.** *Orchestrate* means *arrange*. In the drills from here on, I'll review words from previous Groups to help you understand and memorize them. *Divert* can mean *distract*, and *amplify, augment,* and *exacerbate* mean *increase*.

2. **E.** *Sly* and *furtive* mean *secretive*. *Scathing* means *with criticism and anger*, and *futile* means *useless*.

3. **C.** *Stringent* and *stern* mean *strict*. *Hokey, banal, cliché,* and *trite* mean *overused*.

4. **A.** *Conditional* and *qualified* mean *with requirements or reservations*. *Escalated* means *increased, duplicitous* means *tricky, ultimate* means *the most extreme*, and *surreptitious* means *secretive*.

5. **D.** Make a sentence with the two words. For example, "Covert is a synonym of furtive." Then, try your sentence for each pair of words.
   - A . Ultimate (the most extreme) is a synonym of conditional (with reservations) . . . no.
   - B . Scathing (with criticism and anger) is a synonym of quiet . . . no.
   - C . Surly (rude and unfriendly) is a synonym of mitigated (with reservations) . . . no.
   - (D.) Subterfuge is a synonym of trickery . . . yes!
   - E . Paroled (released on good behavior) is a synonym of stringent (strict) . . . no.

6. **A.** "Escalation (increase) is a synonym of augmentation."
   - (A.) Amplification (increase) is a synonym of exacerbation (increase) . . . yes!
   - B . Orchestration (arrangement) is a synonym of ultimatum (final demand) . . . no.
   - C . Artifice (trickery) is a synonym of hemorrhage (burst of blood) . . . no.
   - D . Chicanery (trickery) is a synonym of honesty . . . no.
   - E . Diversion (distraction) is a synonym of ruination . . . no.

7. **A.** Think of a word to fill the blank, selecting a word directly from the sentence when possible, and then see which answer choice fits best.

   > "John and his fiancée *planned* their entire wedding; they chose the date, made the seating chart, selected the music, and planned the entire menu."

   Orchestrated means *planned the parts to create a certain result*.

8. **D.** If you're not sure what word you'd like to see for the blank, decide if it should be positive or negative. In this case, you definitely want a negative word—negative (rather than positive) remarks might result in her being denied parole. *Scathing* means *critical and angry* and fits best.

Group 3
Clandestine Plans

Find each of the following words on the *Eclipse* page number provided. Based on the way each word is used in the book, guess at its definition.

1. **Judiciously** (p. 11) might mean _____

_____

2. **Interjected** (p. 11) might mean _____

_____

3. **Polarized** (p. 11) might mean _____

_____

4. **Dutifully** (p. 12) might mean _____

_____

5. **Stern** (p. 12) might mean _____

_____

6. **Quailed** (p. 13) might mean _____

_____

7. **Liberty** (p. 13) might mean _____

_____

8. **Clandestine** (p. 13) might mean _____

_____

Let's see how you did. Check your answers, write the exact definitions, and reread the sentence in *Eclipse* where each word appears. Then complete the drills on the next page.

1. **Judiciously** (p. 11) means *wisely*. You might remember the word *judiciary* from history class. The Judiciary is the branch of the U.S. government that includes the courts, and hopefully the courts act **wisely**. Synonyms of *judicious*: astute, perspicacious, sagacious, shrewd.

2. **Interjected** (p. 11) means *interrupted*. This is a cool word to break apart. *Inter-* means *between,* as in *international* (between nations) and *intersession* (between sessions), and *–ject* implies *throw* as in *eject* (throw out). Learning word parts is an amazing way to improve your vocabulary—you have a much better chance of understanding a new word that contains any of these parts!

3. **Polarized** (p. 11) means *clearly divided*. This comes from the word *polar,* meaning *opposite,* as in the North and South Poles, which are on *opposite* sides of the planet—clearly divided. I have seen the words *polar* and *polarized* many times on standardized tests.

4. **Dutifully** (p. 12) means *fulfilling a duty or obligation*. You can determine this meaning from the context. The line before refers to Angela's "unswervingly loyal" friendship. As a loyal friend doing her **duty** for Bella, Angela sat next to Alice every day even though she initially felt a *mysterious* aversion. I must come clean here and say that Angela is one of my favorite supporting characters. Anyone else Team Angela?

5. **Stern** (p. 12) means *serious* or *strict,* and was a synonym for *stringent* in Group 2. *Stern* can also refer to the *back of a ship*, as opposed to the *bow*, which is the *front*. The SSAT loves to test the *nautical* (pertaining to sailing) definitions of *stern* and *bow*.

6. **Quailed** (p. 13) means *felt or showed anxiety*.

7. **Liberty** (p. 13) means *freedom*. Pretty much any time you see *liber-* it relates to *freedom*, as in *liberate* (free) and *libertine* (free thinker).

8. **Clandestine** (p. 13) means *secret, especially for something immoral*. This was a synonym for *on the sly* in Group 2. The other synonyms were *covert*, *furtive*, and *surreptitious*.

Synonyms: Select the word or phrase whose meaning is closest to the word in capital letters.

1. JUDICIOUS
   A. dutiful
   B. covert
   C. furtive
   D. surreptitious
   E. wise

2. POLARIZED
   A. cold
   B. amplified
   C. clearly divided
   D. augmented
   E. exacerbated

3. STERN
   A. stringent
   B. front of a ship
   C. scathing
   D. conditional
   E. tempered

4. CLANDESTINE
   A. surly
   B. abrupt
   C. brusque
   D. secret
   E. churlish

Analogies: Select the answer choice that best completes the meaning of the sentence.

5. Stern is to rents as
   A. bow is to dog
   B. subterfuge is to guile
   C. artifice is to chicanery
   D. cars is to scar
   E. surly is to friendly

6. Liberty is to freedom as
   A. clandestine is to secret
   B. fiancée is to hemorrhage
   C. parole is to orchestra
   D. essence is to ultimatum
   E. vampirism is to duty

Sentence Completions: Choose the word or words that, when inserted in the sentence, *best* fits the meaning of the sentence as a whole.

7. Manuel felt that the voters were _____; they were divided and seemed to either love or hate the candidate.
   A. dutiful
   B. quailed
   C. furtive
   D. mitigated
   E. polarized

8. Anwin _____ when she witnessed the cruel treatment of pigs in large, overpopulated farms, and hatched a plan to _____ them.
   A. quailed . . liberate
   B. interjected . . orchestrate
   C. hemorrhaged . . exacerbate
   D. was startled . . divert
   E. jumped . . polarize

1. **E.** *Judicious* means *wise. Covert, furtive,* and *surreptitious* mean *secret.*
2. **C.** *Polarized* means *clearly divided.* The North **Pole** might be *cold* (choice A), but the correct synonym should more directly define the word. *Amplified, augmented,* and *exacerbated* mean *increased.*
3. **A.** *Stern* and *stringent* mean *strict. Scathing* means *with criticism and anger,* and *conditional* and *tempered* mean *with conditions or reservations.*
4. **D.** *Clandestine* means *secret. Surly, abrupt, brusque,* and *churlish* mean *rude and unfriendly.*
5. **D.** Did you get this one correct? It's a ridiculous question, but I included it because every now and then, the SSAT includes one like this. Here's the trick. The second word uses the same letters as the first, but rearranged. Usually, your job is to define the first word using the second, but if that does not work, ask yourself if there is some other relationship, such as rearranged letters.
   A. Bow is to dog . . . no, they are unrelated.
   B. Subterfuge (trickery) is to guile (trickery) . . . no, they are synonyms.
   C. Artifice (trickery) is to chicanery (trickery) . . . no, they are synonyms.
   D. Cars is to scar . . . yes! The letters are rearranged!
   E. Surly (rude and unfriendly) is to friendly . . . no, they are opposites.
6. **A.** "Liberty means freedom."
   A. Clandestine means secret . . . yes, they are synonyms.
   B. Fiancée (betrothed) means hemorrhage (burst of blood) . . . no. Don't say "For Bella to be Edward's fiancée there will have to be a burst of blood." It might be true, but it requires too much of an explanation to be the correct answer.
   C. Parole (release) means an orchestra . . . no.
   D. Essence (fundamental nature) means ultimatum (final demand) . . . no.
   E. Vampirism means duty . . . no.
7. **E.** "Manuel felt that the voters were *divided;* they were divided and seemed to either love or hate the candidate."
   Look for evidence in the sentence and choose a word to fill the blank. You want a word for *divided.* Then use the process of elimination. *Polarized* means *clearly divided* and fits best.
8. **A.** "Anwin *was upset* when she witnessed the cruel treatment of pigs in large, overpopulated farms, and hatched a plan to *help* them."
   Think of a word to fill each blank and use the process of elimination for one blank and then the other. Only cross out choices that **definitely** do not fit. If a word could work or if you're not sure, leave it. *Quailed* means *felt anxious,* and *liberate* means *free.*

Group 4
Herculean Effort

Find each of the following words on the *Eclipse* page number provided. Based on the way each word is used in the book, guess at its definition.

1. **Congealed** (p. 14) might mean _____

   _____

2. **Federal** (p. 15) might mean _____

   _____

3. **Prerequisite** (p. 16) might mean _____

   _____

4. **Obscured** (p. 17) might mean _____

   _____

5. **Anticlimactic** (p. 18) might mean _____

   _____

6. **Engendered** (p. 18) might mean _____

   _____

7. **Herculean** (p. 18) might mean _____

   _____

8. **Loophole** (p. 19) might mean _____

   _____

Let's see how you did. Check your answers, write the exact definitions, and reread the sentence in *Eclipse* where each word appears. Then complete the drills on the next page.

Definitions

1. **Congealed** (p. 14) means *thickened and grouped.* That makes sense since *con-* means *together,* and *-gel* implies *frozen,* so *congealed* means *frozen together—thickened and grouped.* You can remember that *gel-* relates to *frozen* from the French word *geler,* which means *to freeze.* In fact, when you notice an English word that reminds you of a word in another language, they are probably related, and that's a great way to get a clue to the word's meaning!

2. **Federal** (p. 15) means *national, as opposed to state.* You might remember this word from U.S. History class, and it's a great word to review if you're taking the U.S. History SAT Subject Test!

3. **Prerequisite** (p. 16) means *something required before,* in fact *pre-* means *before,* and *requisite* means *required.* The University of Alaska Southwest is far away, which is what Bella **requires,** and it's located where it is almost always overcast, which is what Edward **requires.**

4. **Obscured** (p. 17) means *hidden.* This comes from the word *obscure* meaning *unclear* or *difficult to understand.* Two high-level synonyms for obscure are *abstruse* and *recondite.* You've now joined the club of fourteen people on the planet who know these words, but that's good because I've seen these words many times on the SAT.

5. **Anticlimactic** (p. 18) means *disappointing. Anti-* means *against* or *opposite,* and *climax* means *the most exciting part,* so *anticlimactic* means *the opposite of the most exciting part—disappointing.* Here's a crazy synonym for *anticlimactic:* bathetic. Have you heard of that word before? Use that in your essay, and I guarantee you'll gain points!

6. **Engendered** (p. 18) means *created.*

7. **Herculean** (p. 18) means *requiring tremendous strength,* like that of Hercules (the Roman mythological hero with super-strength). This is a great high-level word. Standardized tests also love to use the synonym *arduous.*

8. **Loophole** (p. 19) means *hole in the rules.* I included this word to remind you to trust your intuition. If you see a new word that you don't know, but have a hunch about its meaning, that might be enough to get a question correct.

Synonyms: Select the word or phrase whose meaning is closest to the word in capital letters.

1. FEDERAL
   A. congealed
   B. thickened
   C. astute
   D. national
   E. perspicacious

2. OBSCURED
   A. hidden
   B. clandestine
   C. stern
   D. stringent
   E. judicious

3. ANTICLIMACTIC
   A. federal
   B. bathetic
   C. arduous
   D. sly
   E. surreptitious

4. HERCULEAN
   A. legendary
   B. arduous
   C. banal
   D. trite
   E. platitudinous

Analogies: Select the answer choice that best completes the meaning of the sentence.

5. Congealed is to separated as
   A. augmentation is to exacerbation
   B. furtive is to covert
   C. anticlimactic is to bathetic
   D. engendered is to created
   E. federal is to state

6. Herculean is to strength as
   A. ultimatum is to essence
   B. surly is to hokeyness
   C. stringent is to order
   D. parole is to loopholes
   E. conditional is to duties

Sentence Completions: Choose the word or words that, when inserted in the sentence, *best* fits the meaning of the sentence as a whole.

7. The governor warned that the tax _____ must be corrected on the _____ level or else individuals and businesses would have very little tax liability and the national government would lose much-needed revenue.
   A. anticlimax .. state
   B. prerequisite .. surreptitious
   C. liberty .. stringent
   D. mitigation .. dutiful
   E. loophole .. federal

8. Heather discovered that kindness seemed to be the _____ and first step to forming lasting friendships.
   A. liberation
   B. polarization
   C. prerequisite
   D. interjection
   E. escalation

1. **D.** *Federal* means *national. Congealed* means *thickened. Astute* and *perspicacious* mean *wise.*

2. **A.** *Obscured* means *hidden. Clandestine* means *secret, stern* and *stringent* mean *strict,* and *judicious* means *wise.*

3. **B.** *Anticlimactic* and *bathetic* mean *disappointing. Federal* means *national, arduous* means *difficult,* and *sly* and *surreptitious* mean *secret.*

4. **B.** *Herculean* and *arduous* mean *requiring great strength.* Make sure to try all of the choices. Don't just get to an answer that reminds you of the word and stop. Hercules is *legendary* (choice A), but *Herculean* means *requiring great strength,* so choice B is the best answer. Always try all choices and use the process of elimination to find the *best* answer.

5. **E.** "Congealed (thickened and **grouped**) is the opposite of separated."
   A. Augmentation (increasing) is the opposite of exacerbation (increasing) . . . no.
   B. Furtive (secret) is the opposite of covert (secret) . . . no.
   C. Anticlimactic (disappointing) is the opposite of bathetic (disappointing) . . . no.
   D. Engendered (created) is the opposite of created . . . no.
   E. Federal (national) is the opposite of state . . . close enough, and certainly the best of the choices.

6. **C.** "Herculean relates to lots of strength."
   A. Ultimatum (final demand) relates to lots of essence . . . no.
   B. Surly (rude) relates to lots of hokeyness (corniness) . . . no.
   C. Stringent (strict) relates to lots of order . . . yes.
   D. Parole (release) relates to lots of loopholes . . . maybe, but choice C is a more direct relationship.
   E. Conditional (partial) relates to lots of duties . . . no.

7. **E.** "The governor warned that the tax *problem* must be corrected on the *????* level or else individuals and businesses would have very little tax liability and the national government would lose much-needed revenue."

   Use the process of elimination one blank at a time. Cross off words that are **definitely** wrong, leave words that are even somewhat possible, and choose the best of the remaining choices. Also, if there is a word, such as *liability* (obligation or hindrance), that you don't know in the question, cross it out and try without it. Usually you don't need any one specific word to get a question correct! The SAT designs it that way. *Loophole* means *hole in the rules,* and *federal* means *national.*

8. **C.** "Heather discovered that kindness seemed to be the *first step* and first step to forming lasting friendships."

   Prerequisite means *something required beforehand* and works best.

Group 5

Appeasing Charlie?

Find each of the following words on the *Eclipse* page number provided. Based on the way each word is used in the book, guess at its definition.

1. **Exacerbated** (p. 19) might mean _____

   _____

2. **Serenely** (p. 20) might mean _____

   _____

3. **Appease** (p. 21) might mean _____

   _____

4. **Pensively** (p. 22) might mean _____

   _____

5. **Complement** (p. 22) might mean _____

   _____

6. **Avid** (p. 22) might mean _____

   _____

7. **Alibi** (p. 23) might mean _____

   _____

8. **Correspondence** (p. 23) might mean _____

   _____

Let's see how you did. Check your answers, write the exact definitions, and reread the sentence in *Eclipse* where each word appears. Then complete the drills on the next page.

Definitions

1. **Exacerbated** (p. 19) means *increased and made worse. Exacerbation* was a synonym for *escalation* in Group 2. Both words imply that something has *increased*, but *exacerbate* also means that something has *worsened*.

2. **Serenely** (p. 20) means *peacefully* or *calmly*. Fans of *Seinfeld* reruns might remember the hilarious episode in which George's dad frantically shouts "Serenity now! Serenity now!" anytime he gets upset.

3. **Appease** (p. 21) means *satisfy*. Tests love the synonyms for *appease*: ameliorate, assuage, conciliate, mollify, pacify, placate, propitiate. Here's a cool fact for you Twihards out there. In the sneak peak of *Eclipse* given at the end of *New Moon*, this sentence was printed as "placate my dad" and was edited to "appease my father" for *Eclipse*. You gotta know these things if you're a true fan!

4. **Pensively** (p. 22) means *thoughtfully,* like the pensieve in *Harry Potter and the Half-Blood Prince* that Harry and Dumbledore use to watch stored **thoughts.**

5. **Complement** (p. 22) means *amount*. Synonym: contingent. The word *compliment,* spelled with an *i,* means *praise.*

6. **Avid** (p. 22) means *eager* or *enthusiastic*. Synonyms: ardent, keen, zealous.

7. **Alibi** (p. 23) means *excuse*. Synonym: pretext.

8. **Correspondence** (p. 23) means *communication at a distance*. You can see that it has to do with communication since *corr-* means *together* and *respond* means *answer*, so *answer together—communicate back and forth.*

Synonyms: Select the word or phrase whose meaning is closest to the word in capital letters.

1. EXACERBATE
   A. assuage
   B. make worse
   C. conciliate
   D. mollify
   E. propitiate

2. SERENE
   A. pensive
   B. corresponding
   C. augmented
   D. peaceful
   E. Herculean

3. APPEASE
   A. ameliorate
   B. complement
   C. divert
   D. hemorrhage
   E. orchestrate

4. AVID
   A. bathetic
   B. ardent
   C. anticlimactic
   D. sagacious
   E. polarized

Analogies: Select the answer choice that best completes the meaning of the sentence.

5. Ardent is to zealous as
   A. obscure is to microscopic
   B. serene is to obscured
   C. stringent is to clandestine
   D. keen is to exacerbated
   E. pacify is to placate

6. Exacerbate is to worse as
   A. correspondence is to distant
   B. pensive is to orderly
   C. Herculean is to strong
   D. appease is to satisfied
   E. polarize is to congealed

Sentence Completions: Choose the word that, when inserted in the sentence, *best* fits the meaning of the sentence as a whole.

7. An avid coin collector, Winson hoped that the coin convention would serve as the perfect alibi while he actually had a _____ meeting with a secret client.
   A. serene
   B. pensive
   C. ardent
   D. clandestine
   E. augmented

8. With a full _____ of spices at their disposal, the contestants on *Top Chef* were asked to create a three-course Indian meal.
   A. alibi
   B. correspondence
   C. complement
   D. loophole
   E. prerequisite

1. **B.** *Exacerbate* means *make worse. Assuage, conciliate, mollify,* and *propitiate* mean *soothe.*

2. **D.** *Serene* means *peaceful. Pensive* means *thoughtful, corresponding* means *connected, augmented* means *increased,* and *Herculean* means *requiring strength.*

3. **A.** *Appease* and *ameliorate* both mean *satisfy* or *soothe. Ameliorate* even sounds smooth and soothing.

4. **B.** *Avid* and *ardent* both mean *eager.* Remember to use the process of elimination—cross off answers that **definitely** don't work and choose the best of what's left. *Bathetic* and *anticlimactic* mean *disappointing, sagacious* means *wise,* and *polarized* means *clearly divided.*

5. **E.** "Ardent is a synonym of zealous."
   - A. Obscure (unclear) is a synonym of microscopic (tiny) . . . maybe.
   - B. Serene (peaceful) is a synonym of obscured (hidden) . . . no.
   - C. Stringent (strict) is a synonym of clandestine (secret) . . . no.
   - D. Keen (eager) is a synonym of exacerbated (made worse) . . . no.
   - E. Pacify (soothe) is a synonym of placate (soothe) . . . yes, and a much clearer synonym relationship than choice A. Remember to try all of the choices!

6. **D.** "Exacerbate makes something worse."
   - A. Correspondence (communication) makes something distant . . . no.
   - B. Pensive (thoughtful) makes something orderly . . . no.
   - C. Herculean makes something strong . . . no, Herculean requires strength, but does not make something strong.
   - D. Appease (satisfy) makes something satisfied . . . yes.
   - E. Polarize (clearly divide) makes something congealed (grouped) . . . no.

7. **D.** "An avid coin collector, Winson hoped that the coin convention would serve as the perfect alibi while he actually had a _secret_ meeting with a secret client."

   Clandestine means *secret* and fits best. Choose the answer that fits the evidence in the sentence. Winson might have had a *serene, pensive,* or *ardent* meeting, but the evidence in the sentence is that it was "secret."

8. **C.** "With a full _set_ of spices at their disposal, the contestants on *Top Chef* were asked to create a three-course Indian meal."
   Complement means *amount.*

Quiz 1

I. Let's review some of the words that you've seen in Groups 1–5. Match each of the following words to the correct definition or synonym on the right. Then check the solutions on page 171.

1. Subterfuge	A. Churlish
2. Surly	B. Surreptitious
3. Hokey	C. Qualified
4. Covert	D. Artifice
5. Escalation	E. Hackneyed
6. Conditional	F. Thickened and grouped
7. Judicious	G. Make worse
8. Polarized	H. Augmentation
9. Clandestine	I. Clearly divided
10. Congealed	J. Astute
11. Federal	K. Eager
12. Herculean	L. Mollify
13. Exacerbate	M. Secret
14. Appease	N. Arduous
15. Avid	O. National

II. Let's review several of the word parts that you've seen in Groups 1–5. Match each of the following word parts to the correct definition or synonym on the right. Then check the solutions on page 171.

16. Ultim-	A. Between
17. Hemo-	B. Under
18. Sub-	C. Together
19. Inter-	D. Blood
20. Con-	E. Final
21. Corr-	F. With

Neophyte on the Loose?

Find each of the following words on the *Eclipse* page number provided. Based on the way each word is used in the book, guess at its definition.

1. **Transformation** (p. 24) might mean _____

   _____

2. **Neophyte** (p. 26) might mean _____

   _____

3. **Abstract** (p. 26) might mean _____

   _____

4. **Predators** (p. 27) might mean _____

   _____

5. **Coaxing** (p. 27) might mean _____

   _____

6. **Tawny** (p. 27) might mean _____

   _____

7. **Antiquity** (p. 28) might mean _____

   _____

8. **Inevitability** (p. 29) might mean _____

   _____

Let's see how you did. Check your answers, write the exact definitions,
and reread the sentence in *Eclipse* where each word appears. Then
complete the drills on the next page.

1. **Transformation** (p. 24) means *change from one thing to another.* This
   is a cool word to break apart. *Trans-* means *across,* so *transformation*
   means *across forms—change from one to the other,* like human to
   vampire or human to wolf. Another Team Edward or Team Jacob
   moment here. Synonym: metamorphosis.

2. **Neophyte** (p. 26) means *person who is new to something—a newbie.*
   That's easy to remember since *neo-* means *new.* Here's a quick
   quiz about two of television's most famous newbies: In what TV
   show does Dr. Cox consistently refer to Dr. Dorian as "Newbie"?
   And, in what TV show pilot (first episode) did Chuck Bass say
   "Who's the Newbie?" Here's a bonus question: If you've seen the
   Matrix movies, why do you suppose the main character is named
   "Neo"? Discuss the answers with your friends. Synonyms: novice,
   novitiate, postulant, tenderfoot, tyro.

3. **Abstract** (p. 26) means *theoretical rather than actual.*

4. **Predators** (p. 27) means *hunters.* Vampires are, of course,
   predators, but in this case, Bella is referring to large animals, like
   grizzlies or wolves (oops!), that the Cullens enjoy for lunch.

5. **Coaxing** (p. 27) means *persuading in a gentle way.* Synonyms:
   cajoling, inveigling. Standardized tests also use the words *enjoin,*
   entreat, exhort, goad, implore, incite, prod, and *spur,* which mean
   persuade in an annoying, harsh, or begging way.

6. **Tawny** (p. 27) means *yellowish-brown.* A synonym for *tawny* is
   fulvous, but I prefer Stephenie Meyer's choice. "His fulvous eyes" is
   not quite as romantic!

7. **Antiquity** (p. 28) means *the ancient past.* That's easy to remember
   since *antiquity* sounds like *antique* (a collectable item from the
   past), such as the dusty candy dish that your grandma doesn't let
   you touch.

8. **Inevitability** (p. 29) means *unavoidability.* Synonym: inexorableness.

Synonyms: Select the word or phrase whose meaning is closest to the word in capital letters.

1. NEOPHYTE
   A. predator
   B. antique
   C. novice
   D. alibi
   E. correspondence

2. ABSTRACT
   A. tawny
   B. exacerbated
   C. serene
   D. ardent
   E. theoretical

3. COAX
   A. cajole
   B. transform
   C. appease
   D. placate
   E. propitiate

4. INEVITABLE
   A. pensive
   B. inexorable
   C. avid
   D. keen
   E. zealous

Analogies: Select the answer choice that best completes the meaning of the sentence.

5. Neophyte is to veteran as
   A. antiquity is to past
   B. tawny is to yellowish-brown
   C. enjoining is to entreating
   D. vampire is to human
   E. abstract is to concrete

6. Tawny is to color as
   A. red is to yellow
   B. blue is to navy
   C. predator is to neophyte
   D. alibi is to parole
   E. anticlimactic is to ending

Sentence Completions: Choose the word or words that, when inserted in the sentence, *best* fits the meaning of the sentence as a whole.

7. Staying put seemed _____ since no matter how much Emily pushed, no amount of _____ could get the elephant to move.
   A. transformative . . inveigling
   B. tawny . . cajoling
   C. inevitable . . prodding
   D. probable . . artifice
   E. impossible . . subterfuge

8. Noka studies zoology, and his specialty is large _____ and the prey that they hunt.
   A. antiques
   B. predators
   C. vampires
   D. prerequisites
   E. ultimatums

1. **C.** *Neophyte* and *novice* mean *newbie. Predator* means *hunter, alibi* means *excuse,* and *correspondence* means *communication.*
2. **E.** *Abstract* means *theoretical. Tawny* means *yellowish-brown, exacerbated* means *made worse, serene* means *peaceful,* and *ardent* means *eager.*
3. **A.** *Coax* and *cajole* mean *persuade. Transform* means *change,* and *appease, placate,* and *propitiate* mean *soothe.*
4. **B.** *Inevitable* and *inexorable* mean *unavoidable. Pensive* means *thoughtful;* and *avid, keen,* and *zealous* mean *eager.*
5. **E.** "Neophyte (newbie) is the opposite of veteran (expert)."
   A. Antiquity (past) is the opposite of past . . . no.
   B. Tawny (yellowish-brown) is the opposite of yellowish-brown . . . no.
   C. Enjoining (urging) is the opposite of entreating (urging) . . . no.
   D. Vampire is the opposite of human . . . not quite; I'd say vampire might be the opposite of werewolf.
   (E.) Abstract (theoretical) is the opposite of concrete (definite) . . . yes.
6. **E.** "Tawny is a type of color."
   A. Red is a type of yellow . . . no.
   B. Blue is a type of navy . . . no. Notice that this one is backwards; if it had said "navy is a type of blue" it would be correct. Sometimes tests reverse the words. That's tricky if you're not expecting it, but easy for you, now that you know to watch for it.
   C. Predator (hunter) is a type of neophyte (newbie) . . . not necessarily, unless of course you are a newborn vampire.
   D. Alibi (excuse) is a type of parole (release) . . . no, they are both used in a courtroom, but one is not a type of the other.
   (E.) Anticlimactic is a type of ending . . . maybe. Using the process of elimination, this is the best choice; *anticlimactic* can describe a disappointing ending.
7. **C.** "Staying put seemed <u>*certain*</u> since no matter how much Emily pushed, no amount of <u>*pushing*</u> could get the elephant to move."
   Think of a word that you'd like to see for each blank, pulling a word right from the sentence when possible. Use the process of elimination, one blank at a time. Often, it's easier to start with the second blank. *Inevitable* means *unavoidable,* and *prodding* means *persuading.*
8. **B.** "Noka studies zoology, and his specialty is large <u>*hunters*</u> and the prey that they hunt."
   Predators means *hunters.*

Group 7

Insatiable Pull

Find each of the following words on the *Eclipse* page number provided. Based on the way each word is used in the book, guess at its definition.

1. **Redeeming** (p. 29) might mean _____

   _____

2. **Malignant** (p. 29) might mean _____

   _____

3. **Rebuttal** (p. 30) might mean _____

   _____

4. **Coexisting** (p. 31) might mean _____

   _____

5. **Truce** (p. 31) might mean _____

   _____

6. **Genetic** (p. 31) might mean _____

   _____

7. **Transmutation** (p. 31) might mean _____

   _____

8. **Insatiable** (p. 31) might mean _____

   _____

Let's see how you did. Check your answers, write the exact definitions, and reread the sentence in *Eclipse* where each word appears. Then complete the drills on the next page.

1. **Redeeming** (p. 29) refers to *something that makes up for something else*. *Redeeming* comes from the word *redeem*, as in one good quality could **redeem** Heathcliff or Cathy from all their selfishness and evil.

2. **Malignant** (p. 29) means *evil*. It can also mean *infectious* or *cancerous* like when Dr. House uses it. Determining the meaning of a word from its context is good practice. Standardized tests love to use a word with several meanings and ask you to determine how it is used in the passage. Synonyms: maleficent, malevolent, malicious, vengeful, vindictive.

3. **Rebuttal** (p. 30) means *denial*. Synonyms: contradiction, refutation.

4. **Coexisting** (p. 31) means *existing together peacefully*. This is a great word to break apart. *Co-* means *together*, so *coexisting* literally means *existing together*.

5. **Truce** (p. 31) means *ceasefire*. Synonyms: armistice, entente. Okay, let's bring up your SAT or ACT essay score right now. You can use the word *entente* for almost any essay topic. For example, "Formerly opponents, the vampires and werewolves gradually formed an **entente** that prevented any further strife." Just plug opponents from the Cold War, the Civil War, or *Wuthering Heights* into the sentence, and you're guaranteed to raise your essay score!

6. **Genetic** (p. 31) means *relating to genes or heredity*.

7. **Transmutation** (p. 31) means *change*. This is similar to the word *transformation* from Group 6.

8. **Insatiable** (p. 31) means *unquenchable*. Synonyms: gluttonous, ravenous, unappeasable, voracious. Oddly enough, some dictionaries also give the synonym *wolfish*! What do you make of that?! Is Edward calling Bella "wolfish"? Doubt it!

Drills

Synonyms: Select the word or phrase whose meaning is closest to the word in capital letters.

1. MALIGNANT
   A. redeeming
   B. malevolent
   C. gluttonous
   D. ravenous
   E. unappeasable

2. ENTENTE
   A. transmutation
   B. antiquity
   C. complement
   D. fiancée
   E. armistice

3. GENETIC
   A. hereditary
   B. maleficent
   C. malicious
   D. vengeful
   E. vindictive

4. INSATIABLE
   A. serene
   B. tawny
   C. abstract
   D. voracious
   E. ardent

Analogies: Select the answer choice that best completes the meaning of the sentence.

5. Truce is to coexist as
   A. entente is to argue
   B. ceasefire is to redeem
   C. parole is to hemorrhage
   D. armistice is to get along
   E. rebuttal is to start over

6. Rebuttal is to agreement as
   A. redeeming is to arrangement
   B. malignant is to maleficent
   C. coexisting is to warring
   D. coaxing is to cajoling
   E. goading is to imploring

Sentence Completions: Choose the word that, when inserted in the sentence, *best* fits the meaning of the sentence as a whole.

7. Vince hoped that his apology would _____ him after the harsh, churlish words that he had spoken to his manager and best friend Eric.
   A. rebut
   B. redeem
   C. transmute
   D. coax
   E. augment

8. Selma and Maddy have a(n) _____ appetite for attending *Twilight* conventions; they have been to four already this year.
   A. genetic
   B. surly
   C. polarized
   D. serene
   E. insatiable

1. **B.** *Malignant* and *malevolent* mean *evil*. *Redeeming* means *making up for*, and *gluttonous, ravenous,* and *unappeasable* mean *insatiable*.

2. **E.** *Entente* means *truce*. *Transmutation* means *transformation*, *antiquity* means *past*, *complement* means *amount*, and *fiancée* means *betrothed woman*.

3. **A.** *Genetic* and *hereditary* mean *relating to genes*. *Maleficent, malicious, vengeful,* and *vindictive* mean *evil*. *Maleficent* makes me think of the **evil** fairy of that name in Disney's *Sleeping Beauty*.

4. **D.** *Insatiable* and *voracious* mean *unquenchable*. *Serene* means *peaceful*, *tawny* means *yellowish-brown*, *abstract* means *theoretical*, and *ardent* means *eager*.

5. **D.** "A truce (ceasefire) helps people coexist."
   A. An entente (ceasefire) helps people argue . . . no.
   B. A ceasefire helps people redeem . . . maybe, but it's a bit of a stretch.
   C. A parole (release) helps people hemorrhage (burst blood) . . . no.
   D. An armistice (ceasefire) helps people get along . . . yes!
   E. A rebuttal (denial) helps people start over . . . not necessarily.
   Choice B seems possible, but then choice D is a much clearer, more direct relationship. Remember, don't just choose the first answer choice that seems decent; try all the choices.

6. **C.** "Rebuttal (denial) is the opposite of agreement."
   A. Redeeming (making up for) is the opposite of arrangement . . . no.
   B. Malignant (evil) is the opposite of maleficent (evil) . . . no.
   C. Coexisting (existing together peacefully) is the opposite of warring . . . yes!
   D. Coaxing (persuading) is the opposite of cajoling (persuading) . . . no.
   E. Goading (urging) is the opposite of imploring (begging) . . . no.

7. **B.** "Vince hoped that his apology would _free_ him after the harsh, churlish words that he had spoken to his manager and best friend Eric."
   You know the word *churlish* (mean and rude), but even if you didn't you could still get this question correct. The SAT often throws in a tough word that you don't need. So, if you see a word in the sentence that you don't know, try crossing it out and doing the question without it. You'll be surprised how well this works! Choice B, *redeem*, means *make up for* and is the best answer.

8. **E.** "Selma and Maddy have a(n) _big_ appetite for attending *Twilight* conventions; they have already been to four this year."
   Find evidence and use the process of elimination. The sentence does not indicate that their appetite is *genetic* (hereditary), *surly* (rude), *polarized* (clearly divided), or *serene* (calm). They have "been to four **already** this year," so it is *insatiable* (unquenchable).

Ironclad Promise

Find each of the following words on the *Eclipse* page number provided.
Based on the way each word is used in the book, guess at its definition.

1. **Barren** (p. 32) might mean _____

   _____

2. **Derogatory** (p. 33) might mean _____

   _____

3. **Touchable** (p. 35) might mean _____

   _____

4. **Ironclad** (p. 36) might mean _____

   _____

5. **Omnipresent** (p. 36) might mean _____

   _____

6. **Grandiose** (p. 37) might mean _____

   _____

7. **Placate** (p. 38) might mean _____

   _____

8. **Staccato** (p. 43) might mean _____

   _____

Let's see how you did. Check your answers, write the exact definitions, and reread the sentence in *Eclipse* where each word appears. Then complete the drills on the next page.

1. **Barren** (p. 32) means *empty, bleak,* or *lifeless.* If you read *New Moon,* you know that Bella was pretty empty, bleak, and lifeless when Edward was gone. Synonyms: desolate, disconsolate.

2. **Derogatory** (p. 33) means *critical.* Synonyms: defamatory, denigrating, depreciatory, disparaging, pejorative. The SAT and ACT love the synonyms for *derogatory.* Use *pejorative* in your essay, and I guarantee you'll gain a point!

3. **Touchable** (p. 35) means, well, ahhh, *touchable.* If it's that easy, why did I include it here? Because it can also mean *real and definite,* "Freedom was so close it was . . . " real and definite, rather than *abstract and theoretical.* I also included it so I could mention the synonyms *tangible* and *palpable.*

4. **Ironclad** (p. 36) means *definite.* This comes from the iron plating on warships in the 1800s that made them *invulnerable* (not vulnerable) to attack, just like Edward's promise to Bella on page 36 was invulnerable to attack, discussion, or debate. This is a great example of a word that means exactly what it seems—clad in iron, protected, *definite.* If you don't know a word, but can break it apart and have a hunch what it means, go for it; you've probably got enough information to understand the gist of the word and get the question correct!

5. **Omnipresent** (p. 36) means *common* or *present all over.* That makes sense since *omni-* means *all,* so *omnipresent* means *all present—* present all over. Synonym: ubiquitous.

6. **Grandiose** (p. 37) means *very grand* or *extravagant.*

7. **Placate** (p. 38) means *soothe.* You already learned the synonym *appease* in Group 5. Other terrific synonyms are *allay, alleviate, ameliorate, assuage, conciliate, mitigate, mollify, pacify, propitiate,* and *temper.*

8. **Staccato** (p. 43) means *with individual, detached notes, rather than with flowing, connected notes.* You might remember this from your second-grade violin lessons; you play staccato notes by plucking individual strings, rather than playing with the bow.

Synonyms: Select the word or phrase whose meaning is closest to the word in capital letters.

Drills

1. BARREN
   A. desolate
   B. defamatory
   C. denigrating
   D. disparaging
   E. tangible

2. DEROGATORY
   A. ironclad
   B. pejorative
   C. grandiose
   D. staccato
   E. voracious

3. OMNIPRESENT
   A. inexorable
   B. gluttonous
   C. ravenous
   D. unappeasable
   E. ubiquitous

4. PLACATE
   A. redeem
   B. coax
   C. allay
   D. cajole
   E. inveigle

Analogies: Select the answer choice that best completes the meaning of the sentence.

5. Placate is to pacify as
   A. appease is to sparkle
   B. ameliorate is to assuage
   C. conciliate is to coexist
   D. pacify is to interject
   E. dazzle is to mollify

6. Staccato is to flowing as
   A. grandiose is to modest
   B. disconsolate is to desolate
   C. tangible is to touchable
   D. ironclad is to lackluster
   E. omnipresent is to ubiquitous

Sentence Completions: Choose the word or words that, when inserted in the sentence, *best* fits the meaning of the sentence as a whole.

7. Mr. Rodd did not appreciate the _____ tone of Cassandra's comments and warned her of a detention if she continued _____ her classmates.
   A. pejorative .. placating
   B. derogatory .. transmuting
   C. genetic .. rebutting
   D. depreciatory .. insulting
   E. insatiable .. goading

8. The elections board assured the candidates that security during the election would be _____, with no vulnerabilities to fraud or tampering.
   A. surly
   B. grandiose
   C. surreptitious
   D. clandestine
   E. ironclad

1. **A.** *Barren* and *desolate* mean *empty* or *bleak*. *Defamatory, denigrating,* and *disparaging* mean *critical,* and *tangible* means *touchable* or *real.*
2. **B.** *Derogatory* and *pejorative* mean *critical*. *Ironclad* means *definite, grandiose* means *very grand, staccato* means *individual rather than flowing,* and *voracious* means *unquenchable.*
3. **E.** *Omnipresent* and *ubiquitous* mean *common* or *present all over.* *Inexorable* means *unstoppable. Gluttonous, ravenous,* and *unappeasable* mean *unquenchable.*
4. **C.** *Placate* and *allay* both mean *soothe. Redeem* means *make up for,* and *coax, cajole,* and *inveigle* mean *persuade.*
5. **B.** "Placate (soothe) is a synonym for pacify (soothe)."
   - A. Appease (soothe) is a synonym for sparkle . . . maybe to Bella . . . and anyone on Team Edward!
   - (B.) Ameliorate (soothe) is a synonym for assuage (soothe) . . . yes!
   - C. Conciliate (soothe) is a synonym for coexist . . . sort of, but not as clearly and directly as choice B.
   - D. Pacify (soothe) is a synonym for interject (interrupt) . . . no.
   - E. Dazzle is a synonym for mollify (soothe) . . . maybe, again, to Team Edward, but dazzle probably stimulates more than soothes!
6. **A.** "Staccato (individual rather than flowing sounds) is the opposite of flowing."
   - (A.) Grandiose (very grand) is the opposite of modest . . . yes.
   - B. Disconsolate (empty, bleak) is the opposite of desolate (empty, bleak). . . no.
   - C. Tangible (touchable) is the opposite of touchable . . . no.
   - D. Ironclad (definite) is the opposite of lackluster (dull) . . . no. You did not learn *lackluster,* but here is another word that means what it seems, *lacking luster—dull.*
   - E. Omnipresent (all-present) is the opposite of ubiquitous (all-present) . . . no.
7. **D.** "Mr. Rodd did not appreciate the _negative_ tone of Cassandra's comments and warned her of a detention if she continued _something bad_ her classmates."

   Since Mr. Rodd threatened Cassandra with a detention, you know that you need negative words. Use the process of elimination. *Depreciatory* means *critical.*
8. **E.** "The elections board assured the candidates that security during the election would be _invulnerable,_ with no vulnerabilities to fraud or tampering."

   Security might be *surreptitious* or *clandestine* (secret), but that does not fit the evidence in the sentence (preventing "fraud or tampering") as well as choice E, *ironclad,* which means *definite* or *invulnerable.*

Group 9

Chagrin

Find each of the following words on the *Eclipse* page number provided. Based on the way each word is used in the book, guess at its definition.

1. **Indulgent** (p. 45) might mean _____

   _____

2. **Cornucopia** (p. 45) might mean _____

   _____

3. **Catatonic** (p. 49) might mean _____

   _____

4. **Hyperbole** (p. 49) might mean _____

   _____

5. **Flamboyant** (p. 50) might mean _____

   _____

6. **Laboriously** (p. 50) might mean _____

   _____

7. **Distended** (p. 51) might mean _____

   _____

8. **Chagrin** (p. 53) might mean _____

   _____

Let's see how you did. Check your answers, write the exact definitions,
and reread the sentence in *Eclipse* where each word appears. Then
complete the drills on the next page.

1. **Indulgent** (p. 45) means *overly generous*. Synonyms: forbearing, lenient, liberal, permissive.

2. **Cornucopia** (p. 45) means *abundance*. Synonyms: profusion, surfeit. You may have seen this word in Suzanne Collins' novel *The Hunger Games*. The cornucopia is the giant golden horn in the center of the tributes when the "games" begin. The cornucopia holds an **abundance** of supplies and gear that the tributes need.

3. **Catatonic** (p. 49) in this case means *unresponsive and in a stupor.*

4. **Hyperbole** (p. 49) means *exaggeration.* In fact *hyper-* means *over* or *beyond*, so it makes sense that *hyperbole* is *an exaggeration—beyond the truth.* The prefix *hyper-* is a hint to words like *hyperkinetic* (overactive) and *hyperemia* (too much blood). Okay, *hyperemia* will not be on the SAT, but I included the word to open up the possibility for vampire and blood jokes in the drills.

5. **Flamboyant** (p. 50) means *showy* or *standing out,* and literally comes from the word *flaming*, since flames stand out. Synonyms: animated, exuberant. You could say that Edward is **flamboyant** when he stands shirtless in the sun and shines like a million diamonds. One of my favorite items of *Twilight* paraphernalia is the bumper sticker that says, "You take the furry one, I'm with Mr. Sparkly."

6. **Laboriously** (p. 50) means *with much hard labor.* Synonym for *laborious:* arduous.

7. **Distended** (p. 51) means *swollen.* This is a great example of a word you can figure out from the words and sentences around it. Reading before and after the word, you see that Charlie's stomach is swollen from "three helpings" of Grandma Swan's stroganoff that Bella made. Figuring out the meaning of a word in context is a great skill to use on SAT, ACT, GED, and SSAT reading comprehension questions; they always define difficult words in context.

8. **Chagrin** (p. 53) means *annoyance and embarrassment.*

Synonyms: Select the word or phrase whose meaning is closest to the word in capital letters.

1. INDULGENT
   - A. catatonic
   - B. forbearing
   - C. animated
   - D. distended
   - E. grandiose

2. CORNUCOPIA
   - A. profusion
   - B. omnipresence
   - C. truce
   - D. armistice
   - E. entente

3. HYPERBOLE
   - A. transmutation
   - B. rebuttal
   - C. a very large bowl
   - D. lenient
   - E. exaggeration

4. FLAMBOYANT
   - A. abstract
   - B. inexorable
   - C. exuberant
   - D. obscured
   - E. Herculean

Analogies: Select the answer choice that best completes the meaning of the sentence.

5. Laborious is to indulgent as
   - A. distended is to staccato
   - B. arduous is to permissive
   - C. catatonic is to lenient
   - D. Herculean is to derogatory
   - E. chagrined is to pejorative

6. Profusion is to surfeit as
   - A. subterfuge is to crux
   - B. artifice is to guile
   - C. chicanery is to quintessence
   - D. duplicity is to augmentation
   - E. deception is to exacerbation

Sentence Completions: Choose the word or words that, when inserted in the sentence, *best* fits the meaning of the sentence as a whole.

7. Leigh approached the _____ task and wondered if she could find the strength to accomplish such a(n) _____ job.
   - A. laborious .. ironclad
   - B. distended .. barren
   - C. arduous .. Herculean
   - D. dutiful .. defamatory
   - E. grandiose .. tangible

8. The table was covered with a _____ of delicacies, from salads to mouth-watering desserts.
   - A. hyperbole
   - B. neophyte
   - C. novice
   - D. tyro
   - E. cornucopia

1. **B.** *Indulgent* and *forbearing* mean *overly generous. Catatonic* means *unconscious, animated* means *lively, distended* means *swollen,* and *grandiose* means *very grand.*

2. **A.** *Cornucopia* and *profusion* mean *abundance. Omnipresence* means *present all over,* and *truce, armistice,* and *entente* mean *ceasefire.*

3. **E.** *Hyperbole* means *exaggeration. Transmutation* means *change,* and *rebuttal* means *denial.*

4. **C.** *Flamboyant* and *exuberant* both mean *showy. Abstract* means *theoretical, inexorable* means *unavoidable, obscured* means *hidden,* and *Herculean* means *requiring great strength.*

5. **B.** Usually the two words in the question are directly related to each other, and the best strategy is to make a sentence that defines one with the other. However, occasionally on the SSAT, the two words are related not to each other but to the two words below. You can recognize this setup when the words in the question are totally unrelated. In that case, set up a relationship to the words below. Choice B is correct since *laborious* means *difficult,* and *indulgent* means *lenient.*

6. **B.** "Profusion (abundance) is a synonym for surfeit (abundance)."
   A. Subterfuge (trickery) is a synonym for crux (essence) . . . no.
   B. Artifice (trickery) is a synonym for guile (trickery) . . . yes.
   C. Chicanery (trickery) is a synonym for quintessence (essence) . . . no.
   D. Duplicity (trickery) is a synonym for augmentation (increase) . . . no.
   E. Deception (trickery) is a synonym for exacerbation (worsening) . . . no.

7. **C.** "Leigh approached the <u>strength-requiring</u> task and wondered if she could find the strength to accomplish such a(n) <u>strength-requiring</u> job."
   Use the process of elimination, one blank at a time. You can eliminate choice B in the first column, and you can eliminate choices D and E in the second column. That leaves only choices A and C. *Arduous* means *with much hard labor,* and *Herculean* means *requiring strength,* so choice C is best. Choice A is not correct because the job may or may not have been *ironclad* (definite)—make sure to use the evidence in the sentence; you only know that the job required **strength.**

8. **E.** "The table was covered with a <u>variety</u> of delicacies, from salads to mouth-watering desserts."
   Cornucopia means *abundance* and is the best choice.

Group 10
Volatile Wolf?

Find each of the following words on the *Eclipse* page number provided. Based on the way each word is used in the book, guess at its definition.

1. **Interceded** (p. 56) might mean _____

   _____

2. **Pros and cons** (p. 61) might mean _____

   _____

3. **Satellite** (p. 68) might mean _____

   _____

4. **Derail** (p. 73) might mean _____

   _____

5. **Encroach** (p. 77) might mean _____

   _____

6. **Alleviate** (p. 78) might mean _____

   _____

7. **Volatile** (p. 79) might mean _____

   _____

8. **Unveiled** (p. 79) might mean _____

   _____

Let's see how you did. Check your answers, write the exact definitions, and reread the sentence in *Eclipse* where each word appears. Then complete the drills on the next page.

1. **Interceded** (p. 56) means *stepped in* or *intervened. Inter-* means *between* and *ced-* implies *go.* So *intercede* means *go between—intervene. Inter-* can help you understand a tough word such as ***inter**locution* (a dialogue or conversation **between** people).

2. **Pros and cons** (p. 61) means *reasons to do or not to do something.* The pros for Bella visiting Jacob are "doing the right thing by Jacob, seeing my closest friend again, being a good person" and the con is "making Edward furious." Which would you do?

3. **Satellite** (p. 68) means *something orbiting or dependent on another.* Literally, this refers to a chunk of metal in space orbiting the Earth, and figuratively, it can refer to someone orbiting another person. Renee is right: Bella sticks pretty close to Edward.

4. **Derail** (p. 73) means *knock off the track. De-* means *away,* so *derail* means *away from rails—knock off the tracks.*

5. **Encroach** (p. 77) means *intrude on.* I remember this word by thinking of the **roach**es that en**croach**ed the kitchen in the gross house that I lived in during sophomore year of college. Synonym: obtrude.

6. **Alleviate** (p. 78) means *relieve.* This could have been a synonym for *appease* in Group 5, though *alleviate* means *relieve,* and *appease* means *satisfy.* Synonyms: abate, allay, ameliorate, assuage, conciliate, mitigate, mollify, pacify, placate, propitiate, temper.

7. **Volatile** (p. 79) means *unstable.* Paul is unstable; he loses his temper pretty easily, like when Bella first met the wolf pack on the La Push beach in *New Moon.* You really don't want to hang out with a volatile werewolf (I don't mean to take Edward's side, but it's true).

8. **Unveiled** (p. 79) means *unhidden. Un-* means *not,* and *veil* means *cover* (just like a veil that covers someone's face), so *unveiled* means *not covered—unhidden.*

Synonyms: Select the word or phrase whose meaning is closest to the word in capital letters.

Drills

1. INTERLOCUTION
   A. satellite
   B. conversation
   C. chagrin
   D. distension
   E. hyperbole

2. ENCROACH
   A. derail
   B. abate
   C. obtrude
   D. ameliorate
   E. assuage

3. ALLEVIATE
   A. unveil
   B. implore
   C. redeem
   D. coexist
   E. conciliate

4. VOLATILE
   A. laborious
   B. arduous
   C. flamboyant
   D. unstable
   E. animated

Analogies: Select the answer choice that best completes the meaning of the sentence.

5. Derail is to off as
   A. mitigate is to on
   B. distend is to in
   C. placate is to near
   D. intercede is to out of
   E. encroach is to in

6. Satellite is to Earth as
   A. Jacob is to Embry
   B. Charlie is to Alice
   C. Jessica is to Eric
   D. Bella is to Edward
   E. Edward is to Jacob

Sentence Completions: Choose the word or words that, when inserted in the sentence, *best* fits the meaning of the sentence as a whole.

7. Simon is known for his _____ comments, sometimes bitterly disparaging and sometimes praising a contestant.
   A. volatile
   B. voracious
   C. alleviating
   D. derailing
   E. intervening

8. Aware that his daughter was having an argument with her boyfriend, Manuel weighed the pros and cons and decided that intervening would _____ his daughter's privacy.
   A. pacify
   B. placate
   C. propitiate
   D. temper
   E. encroach on

1. **B.** *Interlocution* means *conversation.* Remember that *inter-* means *between.* *Loc-* and *loq-* imply *speak,* as in *loquacious* (talkative), so *interlocution* means *speaking between—a conversation.* If the correct answer does not jump out at you, use the process of elimination. *Satellite* means *something revolving around something else, chagrin* means *embarrassment, distension* means *swelling,* and *hyperbole* means *exaggeration.*

2. **C.** *Encroach* and *obtrude* mean *intrude on. Derail* means *go off track;* and *abate, ameliorate,* and *assuage* mean *soothe.*

3. **E.** *Alleviate* and *conciliate* mean *soothe. Unveil* means *uncover, implore* means *beg, redeem* means *make up for,* and *coexist* means *exist peacefully together.*

4. **D.** *Volatile* means *unstable. Laborious* and *arduous* mean *requiring hard work, flamboyant* means *showy,* and *animated* means *lively.*

5. **E.** "Derail means go off."
   A. Mitigate (soothe) means go on . . . no.
   B. Distend (swell) means go in . . . no.
   C. Placate (soothe) means go near . . . no.
   D. Intercede (intervene) means go out of . . . no.
   E. Encroach (intrude on) means go in . . . yes.

6. **D.** "A satellite revolves around the Earth."
   A. Jacob revolves around Embry . . . no.
   B. Charlie revolves around Alice . . . maybe, he's pretty fond of her.
   C. Jessica revolves around Eric . . . no, maybe if it had been Mike.
   D. Bella revolves around Edward . . . definitely!
   E. Edward revolves around Jacob . . . no way!

7. **A.** "Simon is known for his <u>*varying*</u> comments, sometimes bitterly disparaging and sometimes praising a contestant."

   The sentence tells you that sometimes Simon is "bitterly disparaging" and sometimes "praising," so *volatile* is the best answer.

8. **E.** "Aware that his daughter was having an argument with her boyfriend, Manuel weighed the pros and cons and decided that intervening would <u>*intervene on*</u> his daughter's privacy."

   Use evidence from the sentence—you want a word related to *intervene.* Choice E, *encroach on,* means *intrude on* and fits best.

Quiz 2

I. Let's review some of the words that you've seen in Groups 6–10. Match each of the following words to the correct definition or synonym on the right. Then check the solutions on page 171.

1. Neophyte	A.	Persuade
2. Abstract	B.	Evil
3. Coax	C.	Voracious
4. Malignant	D.	Novice
5. Truce	E.	Ubiquitous
6. Insatiable	F.	Theoretical
7. Derogatory	G.	Arduous
8. Omnipresent	H.	Armistice
9. Placate	I.	Assuage
10. Indulgent	J.	Unstable
11. Cornucopia	K.	Pejorative
12. Laborious	L.	Unhidden
13. Encroach	M.	Intrude on
14. Volatile	N.	Profusion
15. Unveiled	O.	Permissive

II. Let's review several of the word parts that you've seen in Groups 6–10. Match each of the following word parts to the correct definition or synonym on the right. Then check the solutions on page 171.

16. Trans-	A.	New
17. Neo-	B.	All
18. Co-	C.	Beyond
19. Omni-	D.	Not
20. Hyper-	E.	Across
21. Un-	F.	Together

Group 11

Her Crimson Eyes

Find each of the following words on the *Eclipse* page number provided. Based on the way each word is used in the book, guess at its definition.

1. **Loathing** (p. 79) might mean _____
   _____

2. **Proximity** (p. 79) might mean _____
   _____

3. **Crimson** (p. 81) might mean _____
   _____

4. **Vendetta** (p. 81) might mean _____
   _____

5. **Demise** (p. 81) might mean _____
   _____

6. **Macabre** (p. 81) might mean _____
   _____

7. **Bravado** (p. 83) might mean _____ .
   _____

8. **Consensus** (p. 93) might mean _____
   _____

Let's see how you did. Check your answers, write the exact definitions, and reread the sentence in *Eclipse* where each word appears. Then complete the drills on the next page.

1. **Loathing** (p. 79) means *hatred*. "Unveiled loathing" means *unhidden hatred*. Interestingly, "unveiled loathing" is often an answer choice to reading comprehension questions that ask about the author's attitude or tone. But, it is almost never the *correct* answer. Standardized tests favor passages with mellow tones, so the answer would more likely be "tempered animosity" than "unveiled loathing." Synonyms: abhorrence, abomination, animosity, animus, antipathy, detestation, enmity, execration, malice, odium.

2. **Proximity** (p. 79) means *nearness,* like in *High School Musical* when Ms. Darbus says to Bolton, "It's called crime and punishment, Bolton. Besides, **proximity** to the arts is cleansing for the soul." (Disney, 2006) Synonym: propinquity.

3. **Crimson** (p. 81) means *purplish-red*. Crimson eyes—bad. Tawny eyes—good.

4. **Vendetta** (p. 81) means *quest for revenge,* as in *V for Vendetta*. In fact, here are a few extra vocab words from that movie: "The only verdict is vengeance; a **vendetta,** held as a votive, not in vain, for the value and veracity of such shall one day vindicate the vigilant and the virtuous." There's a whole SAT test there. I may have to write *Defining V for Vendetta!*

5. **Demise** (p. 81) means *destruction* or *death.*

6. **Macabre** (p. 81) means *gruesome*. Synonyms: ghastly, gory, grotesque, grisly, hideous, morbid.

7. **Bravado** (p. 83) means *boldness meant to hide something or impress*. The context defines the word; Jake is **"covering the pain"** with his **boldness.** Synonyms: bluster, boasting, bombast, braggadocio, bragging, machismo, swaggering.

8. **Consensus** (p. 93) means *agreement*. This actually comes from the word *consent*, meaning *agree to*. Synonyms: accord, concurrence.

Synonyms: Select the word or phrase whose meaning is closest to the word in capital letters.

1. LOATHE
   A. consent
   B. intercede
   C. abhor
   D. encroach
   E. unveil

3. MACABRE
   A. crimson
   B. morbid
   C. barren
   D. desolate
   E. disconsolate

2. PROXIMITY
   A. flamboyance
   B. chagrin
   C. armistice
   D. propinquity
   E. accord

4. BRAVADO
   A. consensus
   B. accord
   C. concurrence
   D. vendetta
   E. bombast

Analogies: Select the answer choice that best completes the meaning of the sentence.

5. Jane is to crimson as
   A. Jacob is to green
   B. Angela is to black
   C. Bella is to orange
   D. Aro is to golden
   E. Carlisle is to tawny

6. Demise is to destruction as
   A. loathing is to propinquity
   B. abomination is to bluster
   C. animosity is to bombast
   D. antipathy is to braggadocio
   E. odium is to enmity

Sentence Completions: Choose the word or words that, when inserted in the sentence, *best* fits the meaning of the sentence as a whole.

7. Johnny planned a _____ against the television critic for his unflattering and _____ comments about his role in *Five Towns*.
   A. vendetta .. pejorative
   B. fight .. exuberant
   C. contest .. laborious
   D. battle .. Herculean
   E. hemorrhage .. derogatory

8. Si-Shen believed proximity to cadavers was _____, and realized that she did not want to go to medical school.
   A. alleviating
   B. abating
   C. mollifying
   D. propitiating
   E. morbid

1. **C.** *Loathe* and *abhor* mean *hate*. *Consent* means *agree*, *intercede* means *intervene*, *encroach* means *intrude on*, and *unveil* means *unhide* or *show*.

2. **D.** *Proximity* and *propinquity* mean *nearness*. *Flamboyance* means *showiness*, *chagrin* means *irritation and embarrassment*, *armistice* means *ceasefire*, and *accord* means *agreement*.

3. **B.** *Macabre* and *morbid* mean *gruesome*. If *morbid* did not jump right out at you, use the process of elimination. *Crimson* means *purplish-red*, and *barren, desolate,* and *disconsolate* mean *empty and bleak*.

4. **E.** *Bravado* and *bombast* mean *arrogance*. *Consensus, accord,* and *concurrence* mean *agreement,* and *vendetta* means *oath of revenge*.

5. **E.** "Jane has crimson-colored eyes."
   A. Jacob has green-colored eyes . . . nope, brown!
   B. Angela has black-colored eyes . . . hope not!
   C. Bella has orange-colored eyes . . . no, come on now!
   D. Aro has golden-colored eyes . . . no, that'd be the day!
   E. Carlisle has tawny-colored (yellowish-brown) eyes . . . yes!

6. **E.** "Demise and destruction are synonyms."
   A. Loathing (hatred) and propinquity (nearness) are synonyms . . . no.
   B. Abomination (hatred) and bluster (arrogance) are synonyms . . . no.
   C. Animosity (hatred) and bombast (arrogance) are synonyms . . . no.
   D. Antipathy (hatred) and braggadocio (arrogance) are synonyms . . . no.
   E. Odium (hatred) and enmity (hatred) are synonyms . . . yes!

7. **A.** "Johnny planned a <u>revenge</u> against the television critic for his unflattering and <u>unflattering</u> comments about his role in *Five Towns*."
   Use the process of elimination, one blank at a time. If you can't think of a word to fill a blank, you can look for evidence in the sentence and decide if the word should be positive or negative. Then try the choices, and remember to eliminate only choices that **definitely** do not work. *Vendetta* means *oath of revenge,* and *pejorative* means *critical*.

8. **E.** "Si-Shen believed proximity to cadavers was <u>gross</u>, and realized that she did not want to go to medical school."
   Morbid means *gruesome*.

Group 12

Impending Mania

Find each of the following words on the *Eclipse* page number provided.
Based on the way each word is used in the book, guess at its definition.

1. **Deranged** (p. 93) might mean _____

   _____

2. **Utilitarian** (p. 95) might mean _____

   _____

3. **Impending** (p. 96) might mean _____

   _____

4. **Mania** (p. 96) might mean _____

   _____

5. **Exasperated** (p. 96) might mean _____

   _____

6. **Discord** (p. 98) might mean _____

   _____

7. **Plaintive** (p. 99) might mean _____

   _____

8. **Forlorn** (p. 99) might mean _____

   _____

Let's see how you did. Check your answers, write the exact definitions, and reread the sentence in *Eclipse* where each word appears. Then complete the drills on the next page.

Definitions

1. **Deranged** (p. 93) means *crazed.* Synonyms: Victoria is *berserk, frenzied, insane, irrational, unbalanced, unhinged,* and *unstable.* She proves it in the rest of the book.

2. **Utilitarian** (p. 95) means *useful or practical, rather than appealing.* The other fridge magnets might have been cuter, perhaps shaped like sushi rolls or small gnomes, but these two were **practical**—"they could hold ten sheets of paper to the fridge without breaking a sweat." Synonym: pragmatic.

3. **Impending** (p. 96) means *looming* or *coming soon.* The SAT and ACT love this word and its synonyms, *forthcoming* and *imminent.*

4. **Mania** (p. 96) means *madness* or *obsession,* as in *kleptomania* (an obsession with stealing), *Beatlemania,* and *Twilightmania.* How do you know if you have Twilightmania? Answer the following questions: 1) Do you own every piece of *Twilight* paraphernalia, including the Edward Barbie Doll? 2) Do you accidentally call your boyfriend Edward (or girlfriend Bella)? 3) Have you said "no" to others because you are waiting for Edward or Bella to ask you to the prom? If you answered "yes" to two or more of these questions, then you certainly have a case of Twilightmania.

5. **Exasperated** (p. 96) means *very frustrated.*

6. **Discord** (p. 98) means *disagreement* or *disharmony,* like playing two different guitar **chords** at the same time. Synonym: dissonance.

7. **Plaintive** (p. 99) means *sad.* Imagine the **plaintiff** in a courtroom; she or he has been the victim of some wrongdoing and is probably pretty **sad.** Synonyms: doleful, dolorous, forlorn, melancholic, mournful, pathetic, pitiful, wistful, woebegone, wretched.

8. **Forlorn** (p. 99) means *miserable* or *hopeless.* This is described in the line that follows it, "Like he was howling in grief." Poor Olympic wolf, I mean poor Jake. Synonyms: woebegone, wretched.

Synonyms: Select the word or phrase whose meaning is closest to the word in capital letters.

1. UTILITARIAN
   A. berserk
   B. pragmatic
   C. frenzied
   D. doleful
   E. dolorous

2. IMPENDING
   A. imminent
   B. deranged
   C. exasperated
   D. melancholy
   E. mournful

3. PLAINTIVE
   A. forthcoming
   B. dissonant
   C. volatile
   D. grotesque
   E. woebegone

4. FORLORN
   A. indulgent
   B. flamboyant
   C. wretched
   D. laborious
   E. arduous

Analogies: Select the answer choice that best completes the meaning of the sentence.

5. Forlorn is to elated as
   A. plaintive is to euphoric
   B. wistful is to distended
   C. sad is to derogatory
   D. ecstatic is to triumphant
   E. jubilant is to pejorative

6. Discord is to dissonance as
   A. transformation is to serenity
   B. metamorphosis is to correspondence
   C. predator is to subterfuge
   D. novice is to tenderfoot
   E. alibi is to hemorrhage

Sentence Completions: Choose the word or words that, when inserted in the sentence, *best* fits the meaning of the sentence as a whole.

7. Even though she sought simple _____, pragmatic gifts, Corinne enjoyed participating in the shopping _____ at the chaotic, overcrowded malls before the holidays.
   A. deranged .. discord
   B. practical .. vendetta
   C. imminent .. berserk
   D. utilitarian .. mania
   E. exasperated .. frenzy

8. Even eight weeks after the breakup, Bella still felt _____ and mournful.
   A. forlorn
   B. forthcoming
   C. exasperated
   D. volatile
   E. alleviated

1. **B.** *Utilitarian* and *pragmatic* mean *practical. Berserk* and *frenzied* mean *crazed,* and *doleful* and *dolorous* mean *sad.* Interestingly, *dolor* means *pain* in Spanish.

2. **A.** *Impending* and *imminent* mean *about to happen. Deranged* means *crazed, exasperated* means *frustrated,* and *melancholy* and *mournful* mean *sad.*

3. **E.** *Plaintive* and *woebegone* mean *sad. Forthcoming* means *about to happen, dissonant* means *not harmonious, volatile* means *unstable,* and *grotesque* means *gross.*

4. **C.** *Forlorn* and *wretched* both mean *miserable. Indulgent* means *overly generous* and *flamboyant* means *showy. Laborious* and *arduous* mean *requiring hard work.*

5. **A.** "Forlorn (miserable) is the opposite of elated (psyched)."
   - A. Plaintive (sad) is the opposite of euphoric (psyched) . . . yes!
   - B. Wistful (sad) is the opposite of distended (swollen) . . . no.
   - C. Sad is the opposite of derogatory (critical) . . . no.
   - D. Ecstatic (psyched) is the opposite of triumphant (psyched) . . . no.
   - E. Jubilant (psyched) is the opposite of pejorative (critical) . . . no.

6. **D.** "Discord (disharmony) means the same as dissonance."
   - A. Transformation (change) means the same as serenity (peace) . . . no.
   - B. Metamorphosis (change) means the same as correspondence (communication) . . . no.
   - C. Predator (hunter) means the same as subterfuge (trickery) . . . no.
   - D. Novice (beginner) means the same as tenderfoot (beginner) . . . yes.
   - E. Alibi (excuse) means the same as hemorrhage (burst of blood—oops, sorry Jasper) . . . no.

7. **D.** "Even though she sought simple <u>*pragmatic*</u>, pragmatic gifts, Corinne enjoyed participating in the shopping <u>*chaos*</u> at the chaotic, overcrowded malls before the holidays."
   Use the process of elimination, one blank at a time. Choice D is best, since *utilitarian* means *pragmatic* (practical), and *mania* means *madness.*

8. **A.** "Even eight weeks after the breakup, Bella still felt <u>*mournful*</u> and mournful."
   Forlorn means *very sad.* Use evidence in the sentence to choose your answer. You know that Bella may have been *exasperated* (frustrated) and she definitely was *volatile* (unpredictable . . . can you say "cliff-diving at First Beach"?!), but the sentence and the blank are about her being "mournful," which means *sad.*

Group 13

Belligerent Werewolf?

Find each of the following words on the *Eclipse* page number provided.
Based on the way each word is used in the book, guess at its definition.

1. **Capitalize on** (p. 99) might mean _____

   _____

2. **Exuberance** (p. 101) might mean _____

   _____

3. **Ambled** (p. 101) might mean _____

   _____

4. **Catalyst** (p. 102) might mean _____

   _____

5. **Succinct** (p. 104) might mean _____

   _____

6. **Enigmatic** (p. 104) might mean _____

   _____

7. **Belligerent** (p. 108) might mean _____

   _____

8. **Self-righteous** (p. 111) might mean _____

   _____

Let's see how you did. Check your answers, write the exact definitions, and reread the sentence in *Eclipse* where each word appears. Then complete the drills on the next page.

Definitions

1. **Capitalize on** (p. 99) means *make use of. Capital* in this case means *assets* or *profit,* so *capitalize on* means *profit from—make use of.* Synonym: exploit.

2. **Exuberance** (p. 101) means *excitement.* A few lines earlier, the context describes the word. Bella and Jake are psyched to see each other, " . . . too keyed up to sit still in the house. Jacob was practically bouncing as he moved . . . . " Synonyms for *exuberant:* buoyant, ebullient, ecstatic, elated, euphoric, exultant, jubilant, rapturous.

3. **Ambled** (p. 101) means *walked in a leisurely way,* and *ambl-* implies *walk,* as in *ambulate* (walk) and *ambulatory* (mobile, able to walk, related to walking).

4. **Catalyst** (p. 102) means *motivator.* Synonyms: impetus, precipitant, stimulus.

5. **Succinct** (p. 104) means *brief, informative, and clear.* The sentence defines the word, " . . . leaving out anything that wasn't essential"—*brief, informative, and clear.* This is also how most SAT sentence completion questions are set up; the sentence defines the word needed for the blank. Synonyms: compendious, concise.

6. **Enigmatic** (p. 104) means *mysterious* or *difficult to understand.* Synonyms: abstruse, arcane, impenetrable, inscrutable, recondite.

7. **Belligerent** (p. 108) means *hostile.* Often when you see a word that starts with *bell-* (which comes from the Latin word *bullum*), it has to do with something *hostile,* like *bellicose* (warlike), *belladonna* (a deadly plant), and *Bella Swann* (a deadly vampire—just kidding, Bella's first name actually comes from the Italian word for *beautiful).*

8. **Self-righteous** (p. 111) means *with a superior attitude.* Standardized tests love the synonym, *sanctimonious.*

Synonyms: Select the word or phrase whose meaning is closest to the word in capital letters.

1. EXUBERANT
   A. ebullient
   B. succinct
   C. compendious
   D. self-righteous
   E. sanctimonious

2. CATALYST
   A. bravado
   B. discord
   C. dissonance
   D. animus
   E. precipitant

3. ENIGMATIC
   A. elated
   B. euphoric
   C. exultant
   D. recondite
   E. rapturous

4. BELLIGERENT
   A. abstruse
   B. bellicose
   C. arcane
   D. inscrutable
   E. rapturous

Analogies: Select the answer choice that best completes the meaning of the sentence.

5. Amble is to walk as
   A. scan is to stroll
   B. skim is to song
   C. browse is to read
   D. examine is to look
   E. run is to jog

6. Succinct is to compendious as
   A. derogatory is to grandiose
   B. pejorative is to ubiquitous
   C. ironclad is to barren
   D. impending is to imminent
   E. omnipresent is to malignant

Sentence Completions: Choose the word or words that, when inserted in the sentence, *best* fits the meaning of the sentence as a whole.

7. Katniss hoped to _____ the lapse in Cato's attention; she knew that she might not be in such close _____ to him the next time he let his guard down.
   A. jump to . . proximity
   B. exploit . . discord
   C. catalyze . . hyperbole
   D. capitalize on . . propinquity
   E. exasperate . . correspondence

8. To his coworkers Mark appeared _____, offering unwanted professional and spiritual guidance that he himself did not follow.
   A. belligerent
   B. enigmatic
   C. sanctimonious
   D. compendious
   E. rapturous

1. **A.** *Exuberant* and *ebullient* mean *excited*. *Succinct* and *compendious* mean *brief, informative, and clear*. *Self-righteous* and *sanctimonious* mean *with a superior attitude*.

2. **E.** *Catalyst* and *precipitant* mean *motivator*. *Bravado* means *boldness meant to hide something*. *Discord* and *dissonance* mean *disharmony*, and *animus* means *hatred*.

3. **D.** *Enigmatic* and *recondite* mean *difficult to understand*. *Elated*, *euphoric*, *exultant*, and *rapturous* mean *excited*.

4. **B.** *Belligerent* means *hostile*. Choices A, C, and D mean *difficult to understand* and are way out. Choice E, *rapturous*, means *excited* and does not work either. So choice B, *bellicose*, which means *warlike*, is the closest in meaning and the best choice. Even though it is not a perfect synonym to *belligerent*, it is closest.

5. **C.** "Amble is a relaxed walk."
   A. Scan is a relaxed stroll . . . no, they are unrelated to each other.
   B. Skim is a relaxed song . . . no, they are unrelated to each other.
   C. Browse is a relaxed read . . . yes, *browse* can mean *a relaxed read*.
   D. Examine is a relaxed look . . . no, *examine* means *a thorough look*.
   E. Run is a relaxed jog . . . no, the other way around—*jog* is *a relaxed run*. Make sure the words in the answer are in the same order as the words in the question.

6. **D.** "Succinct is a synonym of compendious (brief, informative, and clear)."
   A. Derogatory (critical) is a synonym of grandiose (very grand) . . . no.
   B. Pejorative (critical) is a synonym of ubiquitous (all-present) . . . no.
   C. Ironclad (definite) is a synonym of barren (empty) . . . no.
   D. Impending (about to happen) is a synonym of imminent (about to happen) . . . yes!
   E. Omnipresent (all-present) is a synonym of malignant (evil) . . . no.

7. **D.** "Katniss hoped to <u>use</u> the lapse in Cato's attention; she knew that she might not be in such close <u>contact</u> to him the next time he let his guard down."
   Choice D works best. *Capitalize on* means *benefit from*, and *propinquity* means *closeness*. Choice A, *jump to*, does not fit as well in the sentence as choice D, *capitalize on*—make sure to try all of the choices.

8. **C.** "To his coworkers Mark appeared <u>annoying/hypocritical</u>, offering unwanted professional and spiritual guidance that he himself did not follow."
   Sanctimonious means *with a superior attitude* and works best. *Rapturous* means *very excited* and can imply a **spiritual** component, but does not fit the evidence "that he himself did not follow." The correct answer should work for all of the evidence in the sentence.

Team Switzerland

Find each of the following words on the *Eclipse* page number provided. Based on the way each word is used in the book, guess at its definition.

1. **Pacifist** (p. 116) might mean _____

   _____

2. **Feline** (p. 126) might mean _____

   _____

3. **Parasites** (p. 129) might mean _____

   _____

4. **Tendonitis** (p. 133) might mean _____

   _____

5. **Choreography** (p. 139) might mean _____

   _____

6. **Torrent** (p. 140) might mean _____

   _____

7. **Switzerland** (p. 143) might mean _____

   _____

8. **Incredulous** (p. 146) might mean _____

   _____

56 Let's see how you did. Check your answers, write the exact definitions, and reread the sentence in *Eclipse* where each word appears. Then complete the drills on the next page.

1. **Pacifist** (p. 116) comes from the word *pacific* (peaceful) and refers to *someone who seeks peace, as opposed to violence and war.*

2. **Feline** (p. 126) means *catlike*, like Felix the Cat.

3. **Parasites** (p. 129) are *creatures that live off others, without giving in return.*

4. **Tendonitis** (p. 133) means *inflammation of a tendon,* and the ending *-itis* means *inflammation,* as in *sinusitis* (inflammation of the sinuses). Ben is faking tendonitis so he doesn't have to help Angela address her heaps of graduation invitations.

5. **Choreography** (p. 139) means *arrangement of dancers,* or *fighters* in this case. The ending *-graphy* means *writing,* as in **written** out steps for dancers, like when Haley Graham uses the word in *Stick It,* "I mean who doesn't want to parade around in a leotard getting wedgies and doing dorky choreography? It's delicious." (Touchstone Pictures, 2006)

6. **Torrent** (p. 140) means *outpouring* or *flood,* like the **outpouring** of anger that Bella expected from Edward, or the **outpouring** of milk from Peter's snarf described in the following script excerpt from *Family Guy,* "Peter Griffin: [laughs uncontrollably as a torrent of milk from his nose hits Brooke and Brian]." You've also seen this word in the name of the peer-to-peer file sharing protocol used for distributing **large amounts** of data—BitTorrent. Yep, if you're ever stumped on a word, ask yourself if you've seen or heard the word in Spanish class, as the name of a file sharing protocol, or to describe an animated character's snarf. Synonyms: cascade, cataract, deluge, inundation, spate.

7. **Switzerland** (p. 143) refers, of course, to the *mountainous country Switzerland that has remained* **neutral** *throughout several wars* . . . . And thus was born **Team Switzerland!**

8. **Incredulous** (p. 146) means *unbelieving.* Synonym: dubious.

Synonyms: Select the word or phrase whose meaning is closest to the word in capital letters.

1. PACIFIC
   A. oceanic
   B. coastal
   C. peaceful
   D. bellicose
   E. choreographed

2. FELINE
   A. vampish
   B. wolf-like
   C. dog-like
   D. cat-like
   E. incredulous

3. TORRENT
   A. cascade
   B. catalyst
   C. impetus
   D. precipitant
   E. stimulus

4. INCREDULOUS
   A. neutral
   B. exuberant
   C. ebullient
   D. euphoric
   E. dubious

Analogies: Select the answer choice that best completes the meaning of the sentence.

5. Bellicose is to pacific as
   A. sanctimonious is to self-righteous
   B. compendious is to wordy
   C. feline is to choreographed
   D. belligerent is to utilitarian
   E. plaintive is to forlorn

6. Torrent is to trickle as
   A. cascade is to flood
   B. deluge is to storm
   C. tendonitis is to sinusitis
   D. cataract is to dribble
   E. inundation is to gush

Sentence Completions: Choose the word that, when inserted in the sentence, *best* fits the meaning of the sentence as a whole.

7. Gregory considered all corporations to be _____, taking more than they give.
   A. pacific
   B. parasites
   C. incredulous
   D. dubious
   E. compendious

8. Amrita was a(n) _____; even when angered she would never resort to violence.
   A. pacifist
   B. choreographer
   C. capitalist
   D. catalyst
   E. enigma

1. **C.** *Pacific* means *peaceful*. *Pacific* is the name of an ocean, but it does not mean *oceanic* or *coastal*. *Bellicose* means *warlike* and *choreographed* means *planned*.

2. **D.** *Feline* means *cat-like*. *Incredulous* means *unbelieving*.

3. **A.** *Torrent* and *cascade* mean *outpouring*. *Catalyst, impetus, precipitant,* and *stimulus* mean *motivator*.

4. **E.** *Incredulous* and *dubious* mean *unbelieving*. *Exuberant, ebullient,* and *euphoric* mean *excited*.

5. **B.** "Bellicose (warlike) is the opposite of pacific (peaceful)."
   - A . Sanctimonious (with a superior attitude) is the opposite of self-righteous . . . no.
   - B . Compendious (brief, informative, and clear) is the opposite of wordy . . . yes.
   - C . Feline (cat-like) is the opposite of choreographed (planned) . . . no.
   - D . Belligerent (hostile) is the opposite of utilitarian (practical) . . . no.
   - E . Plaintive (sad) is the opposite of forlorn (very sad) . . . no.

6. **D.** "A torrent (outpouring) is much more than a trickle."
   - A . A cascade (outpouring) is much more than a flood . . . no.
   - B . A deluge (outpouring) is much more than a storm . . . no.
   - C . Tendonitis is much more than sinusitis . . . no.
   - D . A cataract (outpouring) is much more than a dribble . . . yes.
   - E . An inundation (outpouring) is much more than a gush . . . no.

7. **B.** "Gregory considered all corporations to be _takers_, taking more than they give."

   The only evidence in the sentence is that Gregory believes that corporations "take more than they give," so *parasites* (organisms that live off others, without giving in return) is the best choice. He may therefore have been *dubious* of corporations, but that does not fit the evidence as directly, and does not fit the flow of the sentence.

8. **A.** "Amrita was a(n) _non-violent person_, even when angered she would never resort to violence."

   Pacifist means *person opposed to violence*. Remember to think of a word you want to fill the blank before you look at the choices, and choose a word right from the sentence when possible.

The Pinnacle of Safety

Find each of the following words on the *Eclipse* page number provided. Based on the way each word is used in the book, guess at its definition.

1. **Unrepentant** (p. 146) might mean _____

   _____

2. **Pinnacle** (p. 146) might mean _____

   _____

3. **Compiled** (p. 147) might mean _____

   _____

4. **Bowery** (p. 150) might mean _____

   _____

5. **Lattice** (p. 150) might mean _____

   _____

6. **Diffused** (p. 151) might mean _____

   _____

7. **Prosperity** (p. 154) might mean _____

   _____

8. **Aspirations** (p. 155) might mean _____

   _____

60 Let's see how you did. Check your answers, write the exact definitions, and reread the sentence in *Eclipse* where each word appears. Then complete the drills on the next page.

1. **Unrepentant** (p. 146) means *without regret*. Synonyms: impenitent, remorseless. Alice showed **no regret** for holding Bella hostage—she was happy to keep her away from La Push, and . . . well, to earn her shiny new canary-yellow Porsche!

2. **Pinnacle** (p. 146) means *highest point*. Synonyms: acme, apex, apogee, peak, zenith. A great word for the *lowest point* is *nadir*.

3. **Compiled** (p. 147) means *gathered. Com-* means *together,* so *compiled* means *piled together—gathered*.

4. **Bowery** (p. 150) means *like a bower* (a shady place). Synonyms for *bower:* alcove, arbor, gazebo, grotto, pergola, sanctuary.

5. **Lattice** (p. 150) means *interwoven grid*. Synonyms: fretwork, grille, network, trellis.

6. **Diffused** (p. 151) means *spread out*.

7. **Prosperity** (p. 154) means *success*. This is defined in the sentence, "a stable job in a bank."

8. **Aspirations** (p. 155) means *desires*. This is also defined in the sentence; after Rosalie says "social aspirations" she says "social climbers."

Synonyms: Select the word or phrase whose meaning is closest to the word in capital letters.

1. UNREPENTANT
   A. diffused
   B. compiled
   C. impenitent
   D. pacific
   E. feline

2. PINNACLE
   A. apogee
   B. nadir
   C. bowery
   D. grotto
   E. pergola

3. LATTICE
   A. alcove
   B. fretwork
   C. arbor
   D. gazebo
   E. choreography

4. PROSPERITY
   A. escalation
   B. augmentation
   C. exacerbation
   D. parole
   E. success

Analogies: Select the answer choice that best completes the meaning of the sentence.

5. Gazebo is to garden as
   A. lattice is to kitchen
   B. vampire is to coffin
   C. satellite is to space
   D. neophyte is to antiquity
   E. wolf is to moon

6. Acme is to nadir as
   A. unrepentant is to apologetic
   B. remorseless is to unregretful
   C. impenitent is to aspiring
   D. bowery is to lattice
   E. diffused is to spread out

Sentence Completions: Choose the word that, when inserted in the sentence, *best* fits the meaning of the sentence as a whole.

7. Frodo could carry the burden because he was not tempted by the triumph and _____ that the ring guaranteed.
   A. subterfuge
   B. essence
   C. polarity
   D. prosperity
   E. serenity

8. The lawyer had _____ of becoming a partner in the legal practice and worked extra hard to get noticed.
   A. regrets
   B. judiciousness
   C. choreography
   D. tendonitis
   E. aspirations

1. **C.** *Unrepentant* and *impenitent* mean *without regret*. *Diffused* means *spread out*, *compiled* means *gathered*, *pacific* means *peaceful*, and *feline* means *cat-like*.

2. **A.** *Pinnacle* and *apogee* mean *highest point*. *Nadir* is the opposite and means *lowest point*. *Bowery, grotto,* and *pergola* are types of shady places.

3. **B.** *Lattice* and *fretwork* mean *interwoven grid*. *Alcove, arbor,* and *gazebo* are types of shady places, and *choreography* means *arrangement of dancers*.

4. **E.** *Prosperity* means *success*. If you're not sure, use the process of elimination—cross off answers that you are **sure** don't work and choose the best of what's left. *Escalation, augmentation,* and *exacerbation* mean *increase*, and *parole* means *release on the promise of good behavior.*

5. **C.** "A gazebo (a type of structure that gives shade) is found in a garden."
   A. A lattice (interwoven grid) is found in a kitchen . . . no, not necessarily.
   B. A vampire is found in a coffin . . . pellllease! Not these vampires!
   C. A satellite is found in space . . . yes.
   D. A neophyte (newbie) is found in antiquity (ancient past). . . no.
   E. A wolf is found in a moon . . . no.

6. **A.** "Acme (highest point) is the opposite of nadir (lowest point)."
   A. Unrepentant (without regret) is the opposite of apologetic . . . yes!
   B. Remorseless (without regret) is the opposite of unregretful . . . no.
   C. Impenitent (without regret) is the opposite of aspiring . . . no.
   D. Bowery (shady spot) is the opposite of lattice (interwoven grid) . . . no.
   E. Diffused (spread out) is the opposite of spread out . . . no.

7. **D.** "Frodo could carry the burden because he was not tempted by the triumph and *triumph* that the ring guaranteed."
   Prosperity means *success* and works best. Be careful of a choice like *subterfuge*, which means *trickery*; if you are a fan of *The Lord of the Rings* books and movies, you might know that the ring involves trickery, but you must answer based on only the evidence in the sentence. You know only that the ring gives triumph, so *prosperity* is the only choice that directly relates to the evidence in the sentence.

8. **E.** "The lawyer had *hopes* of becoming a partner in the legal practice and worked extra hard to get noticed."
   Aspirations means *desires* and is the best answer. *Judiciousness* (wisdom) can relate to the legal system, but does not fit the evidence for the blank or the flow of the sentence.

Quiz 3

I. Let's review some of the words that you've seen in Groups 11–15. Match each of the following words to the correct definition or synonym on the right. Then check the solutions on page 171.

1. Loathing	A. Accord
2. Proximity	B. Pragmatic
3. Consensus	C. Doleful
4. Utilitarian	D. Enmity
5. Impending	E. Recondite
6. Plaintive	F. Propinquity
7. Succinct	G. Dubious
8. Enigmatic	H. Imminent
9. Belligerent	I. Impenitent
10. Pacific	J. Compendious
11. Torrent	K. Interwoven grid
12. Incredulous	L. Apex
13. Unrepentant	M. Bellicose
14. Pinnacle	N. Deluge
15. Lattice	O. Peaceful

II. Let's review several of the word parts that you've seen in Groups 11–15. Match each of the following word parts to the correct definition or synonym on the right. Then check the solutions on page 171.

16. Mania	A. Walk
17. Ambl-	B. Writing
18. -Itis	C. Madness
19. -Graphy	D. Together
20. Com-	E. War
21. Bell-	F. Inflammation

Group 16

Rosalie's Fervor

Find each of the following words on the *Eclipse* page number provided. Based on the way each word is used in the book, guess at its definition.

1. **Unfathomable** (p. 156) might mean _____

_____

2. **Organza** (p. 157) might mean _____

_____

3. **Lavish** (p. 157) might mean _____

_____

4. **Fervor** (p. 166) might mean _____

_____

5. **Abashed** (p. 166) might mean _____

_____

6. **Vanity** (p. 166) might mean _____

_____

7. **Imprinting** (p. 174) might mean _____

_____

8. **Marred** (p. 174) might mean _____

_____

Let's see how you did. Check your answers, write the exact definitions,
and reread the sentence in *Eclipse* where each word appears. Then
complete the drills on the next page.

1. **Unfathomable** (p. 156) means *impossible to understand. Un-* means
   not, and *fathomable* means *understandable,* so *unfathomable* means *not
   understandable.* Synonyms: enigmatic, impenetrable, inscrutable.

2. **Organza** (p. 157) refers to a *thin, stiff fabric, usually used in
   formalwear.* Picture the thin, stiff, white fabric of a wedding dress,
   or the stiff, uncomfortable maroon frill coming off Aunt Beatrice's
   sofa cushions. That's organza.

3. **Lavish** (p. 157) means *extravagant* and *luxurious.* Anyone remember
   the *One Tree Hill* episode where Jake, narrating during Haley and
   Nathan's rehearsal dinner, says, "On the eve of the Princess's
   wedding a **lavish** feast was arranged. Friends and royalty were
   summoned from lands far away to join the happy couple for a
   night of laughter and magic." (*One Tree Hill,* "Over the Hills and
   Far Away," 2003) That describes *lavish* pretty well. Synonyms:
   opulent, sumptuous. I love the word *sumptuous;* it melts in my
   mouth and makes me think of a **luxurious** triple-chocolate fudge
   brownie.

4. **Fervor** (p. 166) means *passion.* Synonyms: ardor, zeal.

5. **Abashed** (p. 166) means *embarrassed.*

6. **Vanity** (p. 166) means *too much pride in one's looks,* as in the **fashion**
   and culture magazine *Vanity Fair* or the Lady Gaga song *Vanity*
   that begins, "Midnight at the **glamour** show . . . . " Synonym:
   narcissism.

7. **Imprinting** (p. 174) means *making an impression,* literally like
   printing your name on a piece of paper. Before Sam, Quil, and
   Jake, this term was made famous by Konrad Lorenz, a scientist
   who hatched a bunch of geese that **imprinted** on him and
   followed him everywhere.

8. **Marred** (p. 174) means *damaged or spoiled.*

Synonyms: Select the word or phrase whose meaning is closest to the word in capital letters.

1. UNFATHOMABLE
   A. inscrutable
   B. opulent
   C. unrepentant
   D. remorseless
   E. impenitent

2. LAVISH
   A. diffused
   B. sumptuous
   C. feline
   D. incredulous
   E. dubious

3. FERVOR
   A. ardor
   B. organza
   C. vanity
   D. narcissism
   E. prosperity

4. ABASHED
   A. compiled
   B. pacific
   C. succinct
   D. compendious
   E. embarrassed

Analogies: Select the answer choice that best completes the meaning of the sentence.

5. Organza is to fabric as
   A. crimson is to color
   B. Jake is to werewolf
   C. gown is to clothing
   D. bowl is to dish
   E. car is to vehicle

6. Vanity is to pride as
   A. narcissism is to humility
   B. zeal is to discord
   C. imprinting is to dissonance
   D. belligerent is to hostility
   E. exuberance is to calm

Sentence Completions: Choose the word or words that, when inserted in the sentence, *best* fits the meaning of the sentence as a whole.

7. Mike hoped that his irresponsible behavior at the company picnic would not _____ his reputation at the company and hurt his chances of a promotion.
   A. aspire
   B. diffuse
   C. repent
   D. capitalize on
   E. mar

8. Juanita wore her organza gown to the holiday party, the most elegant and _____ event of the year.
   A. enigmatic
   B. imprinted
   C. opulent
   D. macabre
   E. volatile

1. **A.** *Unfathomable* and *inscrutable* mean *difficult to understand*. *Opulent* means *extravagant,* and *unrepentant, remorseless,* and *impenitent* mean *without regret.*

2. **B.** *Lavish* and *sumptuous* mean *extravagant*. *Diffused* means *spread out, feline* means *cat-like,* and *incredulous* and *dubious* mean *doubting.*

3. **A.** *Fervor* and *ardor* mean *passion*. *Organza* is *formal, thin, stiff fabric; vanity* and *narcissism* mean *excessive pride;* and *prosperity* means *success.*

4. **E.** *Abashed* means *embarrassed*. *Compiled* means *gathered, pacific* means *calm,* and *succinct* and *compendious* mean *brief, informative, and clear.*

5. **C.** "Organza is a type of fabric."
   A. Crimson (purplish-red) is a type of color . . . yes.
   B. Jake is a type of werewolf . . . maybe.
   C. A gown is a type of clothing . . . yes.
   D. A bowl is a type of dish . . . maybe.
   E. A car is a type of vehicle . . . yes.

   When several answers work, make your sentence more specific—see if you can define the first word using the second. For example, "organza is a **formal** type of fabric." Now, with that more specific sentence, only choice C works! This is another great reminder to try all the choices and not just pick the first one that works.

6. **D.** "Vanity means excessive pride."
   A. Narcissism (excessive pride) means excessive humility . . . no.
   B. Zeal (passion) means excessive discord (disharmony) . . . no.
   C. Imprinting (making an impression) means excessive dissonance (disharmony) . . . no.
   D. Belligerent (hostility) means excessive hostility . . . yes.
   E. Exuberance (excitement) means excessive calm . . . no.

7. **E.** "Mike hoped that his irresponsible behavior at the company picnic would not <u>hurt</u> his reputation at the company and hurt his chances of a promotion."

   Mar means *damage* or *spoil* and fits best. Always choose an answer based on evidence in the question, which in this case is "hurt his chances of a promotion." Also, make sure the word fits the blank; Mike might be *aspiring* (choice A) to be promoted, but *aspire* does not work in the blank.

8. **C.** "Juanita wore her organza gown to the holiday party, the most elegant and <u>elegant</u> event of the year."

   Opulent means *extravagant and luxurious* and is the best answer. The event may or may not have been *enigmatic* (mysterious) or *macabre* (horrifying), but you have evidence only that it was "elegant."

A Lifetime of Servitude

Find each of the following words on the *Eclipse* page number provided. Based on the way each word is used in the book, guess at its definition.

1. **Import** (p. 179) might mean _____

_____

2. **Servitude** (p. 179) might mean _____

_____

3. **Era** (p. 179) might mean _____

_____

4. **Ire** (p. 186) might mean _____

_____

5. **Berserk** (p. 189) might mean _____

_____

6. **Petulant** (p. 194) might mean _____

_____

7. **Succumbed** (p. 195) might mean _____

_____

8. **Divine** (p. 197) might mean _____

_____

Let's see how you did. Check your answers, write the exact definitions, and reread the sentence in *Eclipse* where each word appears. Then complete the drills on the next page.

1. **Import** (p. 179) means *extra significance*. This is explained in *Eclipse* in the sentence "It was just another afternoon in the garage," with *no extra significance*.

2. **Servitude** (p. 179) sounds like *servant* and means *enslavement*. Synonym: subjugation (being controlled).

3. **Era** (p. 179) means *a period of time in history,* like the **Era** of the Volturi that began when they took power from the Romanian coven 1500 years ago. Synonyms: eon, epoch.

4. **Ire** (p. 186) means *anger,* and reminds me of the great standardized test word *irate,* which means *angry.* Synonyms: fury, wrath.

5. **Berserk** (p. 189) means *crazy,* like the word *deranged* from Group 12. *Berserk* also means *out of control,* like giving someone a new Porsche in exchange for looking after your girlfriend.

6. **Petulant** (p. 194) means *grumpy and irritable,* like in *Desperate Housewives* when Bree says to Danielle, "You don't even know what that means, you **petulant** sock puppet." (ABC, "Art Isn't Easy," 2004) Synonyms: churlish, curmudgeonly, fractious, peevish, querulous. *Querulous* is easy to remember because it sounds pretty *grumpy,* like having a *quarrel* (disagreement).

7. **Succumbed** (p. 195) means *gave in.*

8. **Divine** (p. 197) literally means *Godlike,* but is also used, as in *Eclipse,* to mean *noble and admirable.* Charlie says, "Forgiveness is divine." Do you think Bella should forgive Jacob for his behavior at the end of their last encounter?

Synonyms: Select the word or phrase whose meaning is closest to the word in capital letters.

1. ERA
   A. import
   B. servitude
   C. epoch
   D. organza
   E. vanity

2. IRE
   A. anger
   B. narcissism
   C. eon
   D. fervor
   E. zeal

3. PETULANT
   A. abashed
   B. berserk
   C. impenetrable
   D. inscrutable
   E. querulous

4. SUCCUMBED
   A. marred
   B. gave in
   C. compiled
   D. diffused
   E. exasperated

Analogies: Select the answer choice that best completes the meaning of the sentence.

5. Era is to years as
   A. minutes is to days
   B. year is to days
   C. epoch is to eons
   D. second is to minutes
   E. quart is to gallons

6. Servitude is to subjugation as
   A. ire is to subterfuge
   B. fury is to chicanery
   C. wrath is to artifice
   D. petulance is to irritability
   E. churlishness is to guile

Sentence Completions: Choose the word that, when inserted in the sentence, *best* fits the meaning of the sentence as a whole.

7. Though she was planning to stay in and study, Kalei _____ to her friends' requests and joined them for the party.
   A. engendered
   B. exacerbated
   C. appeased
   D. transformed
   E. succumbed

8. "Forgiveness is divine," Sebastian told Jordan, "and cleanliness is _____, too."
   A. petulant
   B. noble
   C. berserk
   D. pejorative
   E. tangible

1. **C.** *Era* and *epoch* both mean *long period of history*. *Epoch* reminds me of *epoca* in Spanish and *epoque* in French, both ways of describing a period of time. If you did not initially make the link to the word *epoch*, then use the process of elimination. *Import* means *significance*; *servitude* means *slavery*; *organza* means *formal, thin, stiff fabric*; and *vanity* means *excessive pride*.

2. **A.** *Ire* means *anger*. *Narcissism* means *excessive pride*, *eon* means *long period of time*, and *fervor* and *zeal* mean *passion*.

3. **E.** *Petulant* and *querulous* mean *irritable*. *Abashed* means *embarrassed*, *berserk* means *crazed*, and *impenetrable* and *inscrutable* mean *difficult to understand*.

4. **B.** *Succumbed* means *gave in*. *Marred* means *spoiled*, *compiled* means *gathered*, *diffused* means *spread*, and *exasperated* means *frustrated*.

5. **B.** "An era is a lot of years."
   A. Minutes is a lot of days . . . no, it should be the other way around.
   (B.) A year is a lot of days . . . yes.
   C. An epoch is a lot of eons . . . no, they both mean *a long period of time*.
   D. A second is a lot of minutes . . . no, it should be the other way around.
   E. A quart is a lot of gallons . . . no.

6. **D.** "Servitude (slavery) involves subjugation (being controlled)."
   A. Ire (anger) involves subterfuge (trickery) . . . no, not necessarily.
   B. Fury (anger) involves chicanery (trickery) . . . no, not necessarily.
   C. Wrath (anger) involves artifice (trickery) . . . no, not necessarily.
   (D.) Petulance (irritability) involves irritability . . . yes.
   E. Churlishness (irritability) involves guile (trickery) . . . no, not necessarily.
   Choose the answer that is most definite; *anger* may or may not involve *trickery*, but *petulance* definitely involves *irritability*. Remember to try all the choices.

7. **E.** "Though she was planning to stay in and study, Kalei *gave in* to her friends' requests and joined them for the party."
   Succumbed means *gave in*. Kalei may have *appeased* (pleased) her friends by going, but *appeased* does not work in the blank. That's why you think of a word for the blank before you look at the choices.

8. **B.** "Forgiveness is divine," Sebastian told Jordan, "and cleanliness is *divine,* too."
   Noble and *divine* mean *admirable*.

A Companionable Werewolf

Find each of the following words on the *Eclipse* page number provided.
Based on the way each word is used in the book, guess at its definition.

1. **Slovenly** (p. 198) might mean _____

_____

2. **Reproof** (p. 202) might mean _____

_____

3. **Crux** (p. 211) might mean _____

_____

4. **Amenable** (p. 211) might mean _____

_____

5. **Objectively** (p. 211) might mean _____

_____

6. **Peeved** (p. 212) might mean _____

_____

7. **Juvenile** (p. 212) might mean _____

_____

8. **Companionable** (p. 217) might mean _____

_____

Let's see how you did. Check your answers, write the exact definitions,
and reread the sentence in *Eclipse* where each word appears. Then
complete the drills on the next page.

1. **Slovenly** (p. 198) means *messy*. Let's play Name That Quote. Who
   said this to whom, and on what TV show? "I am Preston Burke, a
   widely renowned cardiothoracic surgeon . . . . I am a person that
   cleans up behind myself. I am a person that cooks well. And you,
   you are an unbelievable slob. A **slovenly**, angry intern." Check
   your answer in the Quiz and Review Solutions.

2. **Reproof** (p. 202) means *scolding*. Synonyms: admonishment,
   censure, rebuke, reprimand, reproach.

3. **Crux** (p. 211) means *main point* or *essence* and was a synonym for
   essence in Group 1. Remember from the Solutions in Group 1
   that the magical item that Voldemort used to preserve a piece of
   his **essence** for immortality was called a horcrux. Like Stephenie
   Meyer, J. K. Rowling is determined to help you on your tests.
   Interestingly, the name *Voldemort* breaks down to *Vol* (flight), *de*
   (of), *mort* (death). These word parts help you remember words like
   volatile (flighty, unpredictable) and *mortal* (someone who can **die,**
   as opposed to someone who is *immortal*).

4. **Amenable** (p. 211) means *willing* or *open to an idea*. Synonyms:
   acquiescent, compliant, obliging.

5. **Objectively** (p. 211) means *without being influenced by personal
   feelings*—treating something like an object, rather than like a
   personal matter. Synonyms of *objective*: dispassionate, impartial,
   nonpartisan, unbiased. The opposite of *objective* is *subjective*.

6. **Peeved** (p. 212) means *irritated*. This reminds me of *peevish,* a
   synonym for *petulant* in Group 17. Synonym: in high dudgeon.

7. **Juvenile** (p. 212) means *childish or immature*. Bella felt that it
   was **juvenile** (immature) to be **peeved** (irked) at feeling excluded
   by Jacob and Edward. Wow, Bella feeling excluded by Jacob and
   Edward, that's a new one! Synonyms: naïve, puerile, sophomoric.

8. **Companionable** (p. 217) means *relaxed and friendly*. Synonyms:
   affable, amiable, convivial, cordial, genial, gregarious. I love the
   next page when Stephenie Meyer jokes about her vampires not
   having the fangs usually associated with storybook vampires!

74 **Synonyms:** Select the word or phrase whose meaning is closest to the word in capital letters.

Drills

1. SLOVENLY
   A. compliant
   B. obliging
   C. peeved
   D. messy
   E. in high dudgeon

2. REPROOF
   A. retire
   B. retry
   C. reproach
   D. repair
   E. require

3. AMENABLE
   A. acquiescent
   B. juvenile
   C. puerile
   D. sophomoric
   E. petulant

4. OBJECTIVE
   A. affable
   B. amiable
   C. convivial
   D. genial
   E. impartial

Analogies: Select the answer choice that best completes the meaning of the sentence.

5. Sophomoric is to mature as
   A. slovenly is to sloppy
   B. apex is to nadir
   C. peeved is to petulant
   D. juvenile is to puerile
   E. era is to epoch

6. Stubborn is to acquiescent as
   A. companionable is to pleasant
   B. cordial is to convivial
   C. plaintive is to forlorn
   D. ebullient is to disconsolate
   E. belligerent is to hostile

Sentence Completions: Choose the word or words that, when inserted in the sentence, *best* fits the meaning of the sentence as a whole.

7. When he realized that he had ruined the movie deal, Ari knew he was in for a stern _____ from Eric and Vince for the _____ manner in which he handled the deal.
   A. reproof .. amenable
   B. rebuke .. arduous
   C. coaxing .. messy
   D. reprimand .. slovenly
   E. reproach .. Herculean

8. Velma suspected that the _____ of the mystery and the clue to solving the case could be found in the haunted house where the thefts had occurred.
   A. enigma
   B. discord
   C. crux
   D. dissonance
   E. demise

1. **D.** *Slovenly* means *messy. Compliant* and *obliging* mean *agreeable. Peeved* and *in high dudgeon* mean *irritated.*
2. **C.** *Reproof* and *reproach* mean *scolding.*
3. **A.** *Amenable* and *acquiescent* mean *agreeable. Juvenile, puerile,* and *sophomoric* mean *immature,* and *petulant* means *irritable.*
4. **E.** *Objective* and *impartial* mean *not swayed by personal feelings. Affable, amiable, convivial,* and *genial* mean *friendly.*
5. **B.** "Sophomoric (immature) is the opposite of mature."
   A. Slovenly (messy) is the opposite of sloppy . . . no.
   B. Apex (highest point) is the opposite of nadir (lowest point) . . . yes!
   C. Peeved (irritated) is the opposite of petulant (irritable) . . . no.
   D. Juvenile (immature) is the opposite of puerile (immature) . . . no.
   E. Era (long period of time) is the opposite of epoch (long period of time) . . . no.
6. **D.** "A stubborn person is not acquiescent (agreeable)."
   A. A companionable (friendly) person is not pleasant . . . no.
   B. A cordial (friendly) person is not convivial (friendly) . . . no.
   C. A plaintive (sad) person is not forlorn (sad) . . . no.
   D. An ebullient (psyched) person is not disconsolate (miserable) . . . yes!
   E. A belligerent (hostile) person is not hostile . . . no.
7. **D.** "When he realized that he had ruined the movie deal, Ari knew he was in for a stern _criticism_ from Eric and Vince for the _bad_ manner in which he handled the deal."

   Questions with two blanks are actually easier than questions with one blank—you have two opportunities to use the process of elimination. So think of a word to fill each bank and then use the process of elimination, one blank at a time. In this case the second blank helps more than the first. *Reprimand* means *criticism,* and *slovenly* means *messy.*
8. **C.** "Velma suspected that the _truth_ of the mystery and the clue to solving the case could be found in the haunted house where the thefts had occurred."

   Crux means *essence* and works best. *Enigma* (mystery) has to do with the theme of the sentence but does not fit the blank. That's why you think of a word you'd like to see before you look at the choices.

Group 19

Werewolf Soiree

Find each of the following words on the *Eclipse* page number provided.
Based on the way each word is used in the book, guess at its definition.

1. **Lament** (p. 219) might mean _____

   _____

2. **Somber** (p. 221) might mean _____

   _____

3. **Epidemic** (p. 228) might mean _____

   _____

4. **Soiree** (p. 230) might mean _____

   _____

5. **Exultation** (p. 232) might mean _____

   _____

6. **Consternation** (p. 232) might mean _____

   _____

7. **Analogy** (p. 233) might mean _____

   _____

8. **Dexterous** (p. 240) might mean _____

   _____

Let's see how you did. Check your answers, write the exact definitions, and reread the sentence in *Eclipse* where each word appears. Then complete the drills on the next page.

1. **Lament** (p. 219) means *expression of sorrow,* as in the "Lament for Gandalf" that the elves sing in the first *Lord of the Rings* movie when they believe that Gandalf has been killed fighting the Balrog in Moria. Synonyms: dirge, elegy, requiem, threnody. Okay, be honest, did you know the word *threnody?* Use that one in an essay, and you're sure to gain points.

2. **Somber** (p. 221) means *serious* or *gloomy.* Jacob is **serious and gloomy** for a moment, then smiles and thumps his chest, saying "Werewolf, remember?" Here's your dream reading comprehension question: "Why was Jacob first somber and then lighter in this scene?" Discuss the answer with your friends.

3. **Epidemic** (p. 228) means *outbreak. Epi-* means *upon,* and *demic* means *people* (as in *demographics,* the study of populations of **people,** and *democracy,* government by the **people**), so *epidemic* means *upon the people—an outbreak of disease **upon the people.** *Interestingly, *epidemic* means *lots of people are effected,* and *pandemic* means *even **more** people are effected,* since *pan-* means *all,* like the virus in Will Smith's *I Am Legend.*

4. **Soiree** (p. 230) means *evening party,* from the French word *soir* or *soiree* for *evening.* Okay, let's play Name That Quote again! Who spoke this quote to whom, and in what popular TV show? "I prefer *soiree. Sleepover* is so sophomore year." Check your answer in the Quiz and Review Solutions.

5. **Exultation** (p. 232) means *happiness and triumph.*

6. **Consternation** (p. 232) means *distress at something unexpected.*

7. **Analogy** (p. 233) means *comparison.* For the SAT Subject Test in Literature you need to know two kinds of analogies, simile and metaphor. *Simile is when two things are compared using the words **like** or **as,*** and *metaphor is when two things are compared **without** using the words **like** or **as.*** So "Jacob is like a big, huggable teddy bear" is a simile, and "Edward the sparkler" is a metaphor.

8. **Dexterous** (p. 240) means *graceful and skilled.* You may recognize this word from Diablo II, the video game where you can improve your dexterity (**grace and skill** with weapons) with certain amulets and other treasures. Synonyms: adept, adroit, agile, deft, nimble.

Synonyms: Select the word or phrase whose meaning is closest to the word in capital letters.

Drills

1. LAMENT
   A. epidemic
   B. dirge
   C. soiree
   D. simile
   E. metaphor

2. SOMBER
   A. adept
   B. agile
   C. deft
   D. nimble
   E. serious

3. EXULTATION
   A. triumph
   B. consternation
   C. import
   D. ire
   E. petulance

4. DEXTEROUS
   A. slovenly
   B. amenable
   C. acquiescent
   D. adroit
   E. complement

Analogies: Select the answer choice that best completes the meaning of the sentence.

5. Drum is to instrument as
   A. pandemic is to epidemic
   B. lament is to elegy
   C. simile is to analogy
   D. requiem is to threnody
   E. admonishment is to censure

6. Elation is to exultation as
   A. ire is to wrath
   B. petulance is to abundance
   C. exuberance is to propinquity
   D. macabre is to loathing
   E. enmity is to omnipresence

Sentence Completions: Choose the word or words that, when inserted in the sentence, *best* fits the meaning of the sentence as a whole.

7. Alex went from exultation to _____ when he realized that his chess move did not, in fact, clinch the game, but rather put his pieces in danger.
   A. elation
   B. exuberance
   C. consternation
   D. servitude
   E. vanity

8. Hollywood insiders consider the MTV Movie Awards to be one of the finest _____ of the annual calendar, though they _____ that it only happens once per year.
   A. choreographies . . admonish
   B. ceremonies . . reprove
   C. soirees . . lament
   D. exultations . . loathe
   E. awards . . exacerbate

1. **B.** *Lament* and *dirge* mean *expression of sorrow. Epidemic* means *outbreak, soiree* means *evening party,* and *simile* and *metaphor* are *types of analogies.*

2. **E.** *Somber* means *serious. Adept, agile, deft,* and *nimble* mean *skilled and graceful.*

3. **A.** *Exultation* means *triumph. Consternation* means *frustration, import* means *importance, ire* means *anger,* and *petulance* means *irritability.*

4. **D.** *Dexterous* and *adroit* mean *skilled and graceful. Slovenly* means *messy. Amenable* and *acquiescent* mean *agreeable,* and *complement* means *amount.*

5. **C.** "A drum is a type of instrument."
   A. A pandemic is a type of epidemic . . . no, they are different degrees of an outbreak.
   B. A lament is a type of elegy . . . no, the are synonyms.
   (C.) A simile is a type of analogy . . . yes.
   D. A requiem is a type of threnody . . . no, they are synonyms.
   E. An admonishment is a type of censure . . . no, they are synonyms.

   If your sentence was "A drum is an instrument," then several answers may seem to work. When that happens, make your sentence more specific, such as "A drum is a **type** of instrument."

6. **A.** "Elation is similar to exultation."
   (A.) Ire (anger) is similar to wrath (anger) . . . yes.
   B. Petulance (irritability) is similar to abundance . . . no.
   C. Exuberance (excitement) is similar to propinquity (nearness) . . . no.
   D. Macabre (gruesome) is similar to loathing (hatred) . . . no.
   E. Enmity (hatred) is similar to omnipresence (commonness) . . . no.

7. **C.** "Alex went from exultation to _feeling bad_ when he realized that his chess move did not, in fact, clinch the game, but rather put his pieces in danger."

   Consternation means *frustration* and fits perfectly. Did you remember *elation* from Group 13? It's a terrific SAT and ACT word that means *excitement and happiness.*

8. **C.** "Hollywood insiders consider the MTV Movie Awards to be one of the finest _events_ of the annual calendar, though they _regret_ that it only happens once per year."

   Soirees means *evening parties,* and *lament* can mean *regret.* You learned that *lament* means *expression of sorrow*, which is a noun. It can also be a verb that means *regret* or *mourn.* You can see the connection.

Unsated Thirst

Find each of the following words on the *Eclipse* page number provided. Based on the way each word is used in the book, guess at its definition.

1. **Coveted** (p. 245) might mean _____

   _____

2. **Infestation** (p. 245) might mean _____

   _____

3. **Vigilant** (p. 246) might mean _____

   _____

4. **Decipherable** (p. 251) might mean _____

   _____

5. **Jibes** (p. 251) might mean _____

   _____

6. **Tenor** (p. 252) might mean _____

   _____

7. **Majesty** (p. 253) might mean _____

   _____

8. **Sate** (p. 256) might mean _____

   _____

Let's see how you did. Check your answers, write the exact definitions, and reread the sentence in *Eclipse* where each word appears. Then complete the drills on the next page.

1. **Coveted** (p. 245) means *wanted,* as in the tenth commandment, "Thou shalt not covet thy neighbor's wife." Did you hear that, Jacob and Mike Newton? The other tribe **coveted** the Quileutes' land, and that pretty much started the whole series of events that led to the current situation in the *Twilight* books.

2. **Infestation** (p. 245) means *an overabundance of animals or insects.*

3. **Vigilant** (p. 246) means *watchful, especially for danger* and comes from the word *vigil,* which means *staying awake to pray or keep watch.* Synonyms: circumspect, wary. *Circumspect* is a great word to break apart. *Circum-* means *around,* as in *circle* and *circumnavigate* (sail **around** something), and *-spect* implies *look,* as in *spectacles* (eyeglasses). So *circumspect* means *looking around—watchful!*

4. **Decipherable** (p. 251) means *understandable. De-* can mean *undo,* as in *deconstruct* (*undo the construction—take apart*), and *cipher* means *code,* so *decipher* means *undo the code* and make **understandable.**

5. **Jibes** (p. 251) sounds like *jabs* and can mean *joking jabs.* Synonyms: jeers, taunts. *Jibe* can also mean *agree,* as in *Bella's view of the wolf pack does not **jibe** with Edward's.* Lastly, *jibe* can refer to *a sailing maneuver.* I love the good-natured friendliness (amiability) of the wolf pack's **jibes.** The Cullens have a lot more venom (no pun intended) in their relationships with each other. I'm not committing to Team Jacob here; I'm just saying I appreciate the pack's companionable (friendly) relationships!

6. **Tenor** (p. 252) refers to *the highest male singing voice.* Old Quil was not singing, but speaking in a high, captivating voice, probably almost a whisper.

7. **Majesty** (p. 253) means *dignity.* In previous pages, Bella described Billy's voice as *rich, deep,* and *with authority,* that's *majesty*—like a king, or a tribal elder.

8. **Sate** (p. 256) means *satisfy.*

Synonyms: Select the word or phrase whose meaning is closest to the word in capital letters.

1. COVET
   A. desire
   B. decode
   C. jibe
   D. jeer
   E. taunt

2. VIGILANT
   A. infested
   B. decipherable
   C. satisfied
   D. deft
   E. circumspect

3. MAJESTY
   A. objectivity
   B. peevishness
   C. dignity
   D. fervor
   E. ardor

4. SATE
   A. escalate
   B. interject
   C. polarize
   D. quail
   E. satisfy

Analogies: Select the answer choice that best completes the meaning of the sentence.

5. Circumspect is to diverted as
   A. vigilant is to majestic
   B. vampire is to vicious
   C. watchful is to distracted
   D. wary is to coveted
   E. Quil is to Claire

6. Tenor is to voice as
   A. baritone is to orchestra
   B. color is to crimson
   C. alto is to euphoria
   D. illness is to pandemic
   E. organza to fabric

Sentence Completions: Choose the word or words that, when inserted in the sentence, *best* fits the meaning of the sentence as a whole.

7. Onlookers were uncomfortable when the _____ between Edward and Jacob went from jokes to insults.
   A. laments
   B. jibes
   C. choreography
   D. enigmas
   E. exuberance

8. The meal neither _____ her hunger nor quenched her thirst.
   A. peeved
   B. succumbed to
   C. marred
   D. irked
   E. sated

1. **A.** *Covet* means *desire. Decode* means *make understandable,* and *jibe, jeer,* and *taunt* mean *joke in a poking way.*

2. **E.** *Vigilant* and *circumspect* mean *watchful for danger. Infested* means *with an overabundance of animals or insects, decipherable* means *understandable,* and *deft* means *skilled and graceful.*

3. **C.** *Majesty* means *dignity. Objectivity* means *without personal opinion, peevishness* means *irritability,* and *fervor* and *ardor* mean *passion.*

4. **E.** *Sate* means *satisfy.* Use the process of elimination—cross off answers that you are **sure** don't work and choose the best of what's left. *Escalate* means *increase, interject* means *interrupt, polarize* means *divide clearly, quail* means *show anxiety.*

5. **C.** "A circumspect (watchful) person is not diverted (distracted)."
   A . A vigilant (watchful) person is not majestic (dignified) . . . no.
   B . A vampire is not vicious . . . maybe, maybe not.
   C.) A watchful person is not distracted . . . yes!
   D. A wary (watchful) person is not coveted (wanted) . . . no.
   E . Quil is not Claire . . . true, but not as good as choice C, and anyway, they are two parts of the same person.

6. **E.** "Tenor (high male voice) is a type of voice."
   A . Baritone is a type of orchestra . . . no. If an answer does not make sense to you, it's probably wrong. Never choose an answer just because it does not make sense. Trust yourself; if a choice seems confusing, it's probably wrong.
   B . Color is a type of crimson (purplish-red) . . . no, the other way around.
   C . Alto is a type of euphoria (bliss) . . . no.
   D. Illness is a type of pandemic (outbreak) . . . maybe.
   E .) Organza is a type of fabric . . . yes!

7. **B.** "Onlookers were uncomfortable when the *jokes* between Edward and Jacob went from jokes to insults."
   Jibes means *jokes* and is the best answer.

8. **E.** "The meal neither *quenched* her hunger nor quenched her thirst."
   Sated means *satisfied* and fits better than the other choices. *Peeved* means *irritated, succumbed to* means *gave in to, marred* means *spoiled* or *damaged,* and *irked* means *angered.*

Quiz 4

I. Let's review some of the words that you've seen in Groups 16–20. Match each of the following words to the correct definition or synonym on the right. Then check the solutions on page 171.

1. Lavish		A.	Narcissism
2. Fervor		B.	Subjugation
3. Vanity		C.	Opulent
4. Servitude		D.	Churlish
5. Era		E.	Ardor
6. Petulant		F.	Threnody
7. Reproof		G.	Gloomy
8. Amenable		H.	Circumspect
9. Juvenile		I.	Epoch
10. Lament		J.	Reproach
11. Somber		K.	Acquiescent
12. Dexterous		L.	Sophomoric
13. Covet		M.	Satisfy
14. Vigilant		N.	Want
15. Sate		O.	Adroit

II. Let's review several of the word parts that you've seen in Groups 16–20. Match each of the following word parts to the correct definition or synonym on the right. Then check the solutions on page 171.

16. Pan-		A.	Undo
17. Demic		B.	Look
18. Circum-		C.	All
19. -Spect		D.	People
20. De-		E.	Code
21. Cipher		F.	Around

Review

Match each group of synonyms to its general meaning. Then check the solutions on page 171.

1. Artifice
   Chicanery
   Duplicity
   Guile
   Subterfuge

   A. Ceasefire

2. Clandestine
   Covert
   Furtive
   On the sly
   Surreptitious

   B. Satisfy

3. Arduous
   Herculean
   Laborious

   C. Trickery

4. Ameliorate
   Appease
   Assuage
   Conciliate
   Mollify
   Pacify
   Placate
   Propitiate

   D. Abundance

5. Armistice
   Entente
   Truce

   E. Highest point

6. Cornucopia
   Profusion
   Surfeit

   F. Secret

7. Acme
   Apex
   Apogee
   Peak
   Pinnacle
   Zenith

   G. Requiring tremendous strength

Group 21
Mutually Inclusive?

Find each of the following words on the *Eclipse* page number provided. Based on the way each word is used in the book, guess at its definition.

1. **Adulation** (p. 260) might mean _____

_____

2. **Abstraction** (p. 270) might mean _____

_____

3. **Reconcile** (p. 271) might mean _____

_____

4. **Obtuse** (p. 274) might mean _____

_____

5. **Scarlet** (p. 275) might mean _____

_____

6. **Paroxysms** (p. 276) might mean _____

_____

7. **Connotations** (p. 277) might mean _____

_____

8. **Mutually exclusive** (p. 277) might mean _____

_____

Let's see how you did. Check your answers, write the exact definitions,
and reread the sentence in *Eclipse* where each word appears. Then
complete the drills on the next page.

1. **Adulation** (p. 260) means *extreme admiration*. Synonym:
   veneration.

2. **Abstraction** (p. 270) means *distracted thinking* and comes from the
   word *abstract,* meaning *conceptual (related to **thoughts**) rather than
   actual.* Synonym: woolgathering.

3. **Reconcile** (p. 271) means *settle.* Remember from Group 8 that
   conciliate was a synonym for *placate,* meaning *soothe.* Since *re-*
   means *again,* re**concile** sounds like *soothe again—settle.*

4. **Obtuse** (p. 274) means *thick, slow to comprehend.* I can always count
   on Edward to use a great SAT word like *obtuse.* Bella uses pretty
   excellent words, too, like *belligerent* and *petulant.*

5. **Scarlet** (p. 275) means *bright red.* Interestingly, *scarlet* can also
   mean *heinous* (wicked), *immoral,* and *promiscuous* (unchaste, sexually
   liberal), like when Ron says to Hermione on page 513 in *Harry
   Potter and the Goblet of Fire,* "I told you not to annoy Rita Skeeter!
   She's made you out to be some sort of—scarlet woman!"

6. **Paroxysms** (p. 276) means *attacks, usually of an emotion or activity,
   such as laughter or crying. Para-* means *beyond,* as in *paranormal*
   (beyond normal), and *-oxysm* implies *sharpen,* so *paroxysm* means
   sharpen beyond normal laughter—an ***intense, focused*** burst of
   laughter.

7. **Connotations** (p. 277) means *implications.* When Edward was
   human, *eternity* did not **imply** the same thing that it does now. It
   was *abstract* (a concept, not literal), but now that he's immortal, it
   is *literal* (actual). By the way, this is a sweet passage in *Eclipse.* Did
   you need a tissue?

8. **Mutually exclusive** (p. 277) means *unable to occur at the same time.*
   I have seen this expression many times on standardized tests. For
   Bella, choosing Edward and choosing Jacob are mutually exclusive
   events; they can't both occur at the same time. Or can they?

88 **Synonyms:** Select the word or phrase whose meaning is closest to the word in capital letters.

1. ADULATION
   A. abstraction
   B. woolgathering
   C. vigilance
   D. veneration
   E. jibes

2. RECONCILE
   A. settle
   B. covet
   C. decipher
   D. sate
   E. succumb

3. OBTUSE
   A. scarlet
   B. mutually exclusive
   C. thick
   D. majestic
   E. circumspect

4. CONNOTATION
   A. implication
   B. cornucopia
   C. profusion
   D. surfeit
   E. hyperbole

Analogies: Select the answer choice that best completes the meaning of the sentence.

5. Paroxysm is to laughter as
   A. adulation is to censure
   B. abstraction is to focus
   C. exultation is to forlornness
   D. torrent is to water
   E. consternation is to appeasement

6. Obtuse is to comprehend as
   A. circumspect is to watch
   B. dexterous is to move
   C. ambling is to mar
   D. nimble is to run
   E. acquiescent is to argue

Sentence Completions: Choose the word or words that, when inserted in the sentence, *best* fits the meaning of the sentence as a whole.

7. Once the scientists realized that carbon and hydrogen were not _____ a solution, they presented the _____ of such a discovery in academic journals.
   A. the crux of .. paroxysms
   B. mutually exclusive to .. implications
   C. reconciled with .. connotations
   D. venerated by .. obtuseness
   E. required of .. abstraction

8. Mortified, Peyton went _____ when Lucas made a revealing toast at the wedding.
   A. obtuse
   B. circumspect
   C. adroit
   D. agile
   E. scarlet

1. **D.** *Adulation* and *veneration* mean *extreme admiration. Abstraction* and *woolgathering* mean *distracted thinking, vigilance* means *watchfulness,* and *jibes* means *jokes.*

2. **A.** *Reconcile* means *settle. Covet* means *want, decipher* means *decode, sate* means *satisfy,* and *succumb* means *give in.*
3. **C.** *Obtuse* means *thick. Scarlet* is *bright red, mutually exclusive* means *not occurring at the same time, majestic* means *dignified,* and *circumspect* means *watchful for danger.*
4. **A.** *Connotation* means *implication. Cornucopia, profusion,* and *surfeit* mean *abundance. Hyperbole* means *exaggeration.*
5. **D.** "Paroxysm (attack of emotion or laughter) is lots of laughter."
   - A. Adulation (extreme admiration) is lots of censure (criticism) . . . no.
   - B. Abstraction (distracted thinking) is lots of focus . . . no.
   - C. Exultation (happiness) is lots of forlornness (sadness) . . . no.
   - (D.) Torrent (gush of water) is lots of water . . . yes.
   - E. Consternation (frustration) is lots of appeasement (soothing) . . . no.
6. **E.** "An obtuse person is slow to comprehend."
   - A. A circumspect (watchful) person is slow to watch . . . no.
   - B. A dexterous (graceful) person is slow to move . . . no.
   - C. An ambling (walking in a relaxed way) person is slow to mar (spoil) . . . no.
   - D. A nimble (graceful) person is slow to run . . . no.
   - (E.) An acquiescent (accommodating) person is slow to argue . . . yes, an accommodating person is less likely to argue.
7. **B.** "Once the scientists realized that carbon and hydrogen were not *????* a solution, they presented the *????* of such a discovery in academic journals."

   Occasionally, you might not be able to use a word from the sentence or even think of a word to fill the blank. If that happens, try the answer choices for the blank and use the process of elimination. Make sure the word fits the evidence in the sentence. Only choice B fits the blanks, the flow of the sentence, and the evidence.
8. **E.** "Mortified, Peyton went *mortified* when Lucas made a revealing toast at the wedding."

   Scarlet implies *blushing* and works best with the evidence "mortified" and "revealing toast."

Group 22
Transitory Customs

Find each of the following words on the *Eclipse* page number provided. Based on the way each word is used in the book, guess at its definition.

1. **Transitory** (p. 278) might mean _____

   _____

2. **Dirge** (p. 278) might mean _____

   _____

3. **Prolific** (p. 279) might mean _____

   _____

4. **Beleaguered** (p. 279) might mean _____

   _____

5. **Reluctant** (p. 279) might mean _____

   _____

6. **Carnage** (p. 279) might mean _____

   _____

7. **Homicides** (p. 279) might mean _____

   _____

8. **Rampage** (p. 279) might mean _____

   _____

1. **Transitory** (p. 278) means *temporary*. Synonyms: ephemeral, evanescent, fleeting, impermanent, transient. These are some great standardized test vocabulary words and remind me of the band *Evanescence,* which means *impermanence*, and according to the lead singer, was named for the mysterious image the name conjures.

2. **Dirge** (p. 278) means *expression of mourning, like a song or poem at a funeral* and was a synonym for *lament* in Group 19. The other synonyms were *elegy*, *requiem*, and *threnody*.

3. **Prolific** (p. 279) means *producing many works, abundant,* or *widespread*. To call the serial killer *prolific* means he killed **many** people. You can see this in the next line, ". . . convicted of the murders of 48 women." Eek! Synonyms: bountiful, copious, fecund, plenteous, profuse.

4. **Beleaguered** (p. 279) means *troubled* or *attacked*. Synonym: besieged.

5. **Reluctant** (p. 279) means *hesitant*.

6. **Carnage** (p. 279) means *killing,* from the prefix *carn-* which means *flesh,* as in *carnivorous* (flesh eating).

7. **Homicides** (p. 279) means *murders.* You already know this word from police shows like *CSI* and *NCIS*. This is a great word to break apart. *Homo-* in this case means *human,* as in *homo sapiens (human beings),* and *-cide* means *killing,* as in *genocide* (killing of a racial group) and *insecticide* (killing of insects), so *homicide* means *killing of humans.*

8. **Rampage** (p. 279) means *out-of-control behavior,* like when Homer loses it in *The Simpsons* episode "Treehouse of Horror V," and Marge radios for help, "Husband on murderous **rampage.** Send help. Over." (Fox, *The Simpsons,* "Treehouse of Horror V," 1989) Rampage is also the name of the **raging psychopathic** Decepticon Transformer.

Synonyms: Select the word or phrase whose meaning is closest to the word in capital letters.

1. TRANSITORY
   A. prolific
   B. ephemeral
   C. copious
   D. fecund
   E. profuse

2. DIRGE
   A. threnody
   B. rampage
   C. homicide
   D. genocide
   E. carnage

3. PROLIFIC
   A. obtuse
   B. scarlet
   C. vigilant
   D. bountiful
   E. adroit

4. BELEAGUERED
   A. troubled
   B. serene
   C. appeased
   D. pensive
   E. engendered

Analogies: Select the answer choice that best completes the meaning of the sentence.

5. Transient is to permanent as
   A. reluctant is to hesitant
   B. abstract is to literal
   C. objective is to unbiased
   D. puerile is to sophomoric
   E. somber is to serious

6. Detective is to homicides as
   A. vampire is to blood
   B. werewolf is to transformations
   C. sheriff is to reluctance
   D. choreographer is to dance steps
   E. director is to carnage

Sentence Completions: Choose the word that, when inserted in the sentence, *best* fits the meaning of the sentence as a whole.

7. Beleaguered by repeated attacks of rampaging elephants, the villagers were reluctant to stay in the village, and considered moving temporarily to their _____ winter retreat in the south.
   A. prolific
   B. transient
   C. fecund
   D. profuse
   E. obtuse

8. Fans feel that Chester French's new keyboard player has the innovative talent, creativity, energy, and drive that will make him one of the most _____ keyboard players of all time.
   A. evanescent
   B. beleaguered
   C. homicidal
   D. prolific
   E. rampaging

1. **B.** *Transitory* and *ephemeral* mean *temporary. Prolific, copious, fecund,* and *profuse* mean *widespread* and *abundant.*

2. **A.** *Dirge* and *threnody* mean *lament* or *funeral song. Rampage* means *out-of-control behavior,* which could result in a *homicide* (murder), which could result in a *funeral song,* but is not the definition of *dirge.* The correct choice should have a much clearer and more direct relationship. *Genocide* means *killing of an ethnic group,* and *carnage* means *killing.*

3. **D.** *Prolific* means *bountiful. Obtuse* means *thick, scarlet* means *bright red, vigilant* means *watchful,* and *adroit* means *skilled and graceful.*

4. **A.** *Beleaguered* means *troubled. Serene* means *calm, appeased* means *pleased, pensive* means *thoughtful,* and *engendered* means *caused.*

5. **B.** "Transient is the opposite of permanent."
   A. Reluctant (hesitant) is the opposite of hesitant . . . no.
   B. Abstract (theoretical) is the opposite of literal . . . yes!
   C. Objective (unbiased) is the opposite of unbiased . . . no.
   D. Puerile (immature) is the opposite of sophomoric (immature) . . . no.
   E. Somber (serious) is the opposite of serious . . . no.

6. **D.** "A detective investigates/works on homicides."
   A. A vampire investigates/works on blood . . . maybe, but it's a weak answer.
   B. A werewolf investigates/works on transformations . . . not quite.
   C. A sheriff investigates/works on reluctance . . . no. Don't convince yourself that a sheriff deals with criminals who are reluctant to give info and confess. If you can't make a clear link in one short sentence, then it's not the correct answer.
   D. A choreographer investigates/works on dance steps . . . yes!
   E. A director investigates/works on carnage . . . no, unless you're talking about the zombie flicks that Bella sought out in *New Moon.*
   Choice D is best.

7. **B.** "Beleaguered by repeated attacks of rampaging elephants, the villagers were reluctant to stay in the village, and considered moving temporarily to their *temporary* winter retreat in the south."
   Use the process of elimination. *Transient* means *temporary* and fits best.

8. **D.** "Fans feel that Chester French's new keyboard player has the innovative talent, creativity, energy, and drive that will make him one of the most *driven* keyboard players of all time."
   Look for evidence, and when possible, use a word directly from the sentence to fill the blank. Then go to the choices. *Prolific* means *productive* and fits best.

Prophecy

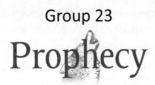

Find each of the following words on the *Eclipse* page number provided. Based on the way each word is used in the book, guess at its definition.

1. **Diverse** (p. 280) might mean _____

   _____

2. **Modus operandi** (p. 280) might mean _____

   _____

3. **Conflagrations** (p. 280) might mean _____

   _____

4. **Accelerant** (p. 280) might mean _____

   _____

5. **Concealment** (p. 280) might mean _____

   _____

6. **Indisputable** (p. 281) might mean _____

   _____

7. **Prophecy** (p. 282) might mean _____

   _____

8. **Pessimist** (p. 284) might mean _____

   _____

Let's see how you did. Check your answers, write the exact definitions,
and reread the sentence in *Eclipse* where each word appears. Then
complete the drills on the next page.

1. **Diverse** (p. 280) means *varied.* In *Eclipse,* the word *diverse* is
   followed by a colon, and then a list of examples that demonstrate
   the diversity. That's exactly how many SAT sentence completion
   questions are set up; *diverse* would be replaced by a blank, and
   the examples would demonstrate what you would need to fill the
   blank. Synonyms: heterogeneous, manifold, motley, multifarious,
   sundry, variegated. That is a terrific list of synonyms; I have seen
   almost every one of those words on tests. Memorize them and
   your score will go up!

2. **Modus operandi** (p. 280) means *way of doing something.* It
   translates from Latin as *way of operating.* You hear this in crime
   shows when a detective or lawyer asks, "Does the defendant's MO
   (the abbreviation for *modus operandi*) match at both crime scenes?"
   Synonym: methodology.

3. **Conflagrations** (p. 280) means *fires.* This is a great word to break
   apart. *Con-* means *with,* and *flagrat* implies *fire,* as in the spell
   Flagrate, which Hermione used to cast a glowing, **fiery** mark on
   doors in the Department of Mysteries in *Harry Potter and the Order
   of the Phoenix.*

4. **Accelerant** (p. 280) is a chemistry word for *something that accelerates
   (speeds up) the spread of fire.* It can also refer to *anything that speeds
   things up.* Synonym: catalyst.

5. **Concealment** (p. 280) means *hiding.*

6. **Indisputable** (p. 281) means *not disputable—definite.*

7. **Prophecy** (p. 282) means *prediction.* In an unrelated note, here's
   some cool *Twilight* trivia. Did you notice that on the next page
   Bella refers to Emmett as Edward's "favorite brother." How do
   you feel about that? It makes sense, and maybe you could have
   guessed it, but it was never stated directly before.

8. **Pessimist** (p. 284) means *someone who imagines that bad things will
   happen.* The opposite is an *optimist.*

Synonyms: Select the word or phrase whose meaning is closest to the word in capital letters.

1. DIVERSE
   A. accelerated
   B. concealed
   C. pessimistic
   D. multifarious
   E. reluctant

2. CONFLAGRATION
   A. fire
   B. homicide
   C. rampage
   D. carnage
   E. dirge

3. INDISPUTABLE
   A. ephemeral
   B. evanescent
   C. fleeting
   D. transient
   E. definite

4. PROPHECY
   A. elegy
   B. prediction
   C. requiem
   D. lament
   E. threnody

Analogies: Select the answer choice that best completes the meaning of the sentence.

5. Diverse is to unvaried as
   A. heterogeneous is to indisputable
   B. motley is to alike
   C. manifold is to prolific
   D. multifarious is to bountiful
   E. sundry is to fecund

6. Pessimistic is to bad as
   A. reluctant is to somber
   B. beleaguered is to epidemic
   C. obtuse is to petulant
   D. circumspect is to dangerous
   E. sophomoric is to unfathomable

Sentence Completions: Choose the word that, when inserted in the sentence, *best* fits the meaning of the sentence as a whole.

7. Special Agent Gibbs noted that the MO suggested by evidence at the crime scene exactly matched the _____ used to break into the Navy shipyard three years earlier.
   A. diversity
   B. variegation
   C. catalyst
   D. accelerant
   E. methodology

8. According to the _____, a hero would arise and lead the people to freedom; but many people doubted such predictions and considered them foolish legends.
   A. conflagrations
   B. libertines
   C. doubts
   D. prophecies
   E. torrents

1. **D.** *Diverse* and *multifarious* mean *varied*. *Multifarious* also implies *many* as well as *varied*. *Accelerated* means *sped up,* *concealed* means *hidden,* *pessimistic* means *expecting bad things to happen,* and *reluctant* means *hesitant.*

2. **A.** *Conflagration* means *fire.* *Homicide* means *murder,* *rampage* means *out-of-control behavior,* *carnage* means *killing,* and *dirge* means *expression of sorrow.*
3. **E.** *Indisputable* means *definite.* *Ephemeral, evanescent, fleeting,* and *transient* mean *temporary.*
4. **B.** *Prophecy* means *prediction.* *Elegy, requiem, lament,* and *threnody* mean *expression of sorrow.*
5. **B.** "Diverse (varied) is the opposite of unvaried."
   A. Heterogeneous (varied) is the opposite of indisputable (definite) . . . maybe, but it's a big stretch.
   B. Motley (varied) is the opposite of alike . . . yes.
   C. Manifold (many and varied) is the opposite of prolific (abundant) . . . no.
   D. Multifarious (many and varied) is the opposite of bountiful (abundant) . . . no.
   E. Sundry (varied) is the opposite of fecund (abundant) . . . no.
6. **D.** "A pessimistic person expects bad things."
   A. A reluctant (hesitant) person expects somber (serious) things . . . maybe, but a hesitant person could expect silly or serious things.
   B. A beleaguered (attacked) person expects epidemic (widespread disease) things . . . maybe.
   C. An obtuse (thick) person expects petulant (irritable) things . . . no, not necessarily.
   D. A circumspect (wary) person expects dangerous things . . . yes, *circumspect* means *watchful for* **danger.**
   E. A sophomoric (immature) person expects unfathomable things . . . no, not necessarily.
7. **E.** "Special Agent Gibbs noted that the MO suggested by evidence at the crime scene exactly matched the _MO_ used to break into the Navy shipyard three years earlier."
   Methodology and *MO (modus operandi)* mean *way of doing something.*
8. **D.** "According to the _predictions_, a hero would arise and lead the people to freedom; but many people doubted such predictions and considered them foolish legends."

   Think of a word you'd like to see, taking a word or words right from the sentence when possible and then use the process of elimination. *Prophecies* means *predictions.*

Circumspect Comrades

Find each of the following words on the *Eclipse* page number provided. Based on the way each word is used in the book, guess at its definition.

1. **Appalled** (p. 287) might mean _____

    _____

2. **Anonymity** (p. 289) might mean _____

    _____

3. **Proportions** (p. 290) might mean _____

    _____

4. **Circumspectly** (p. 292) might mean _____

    _____

5. **Wane** (p. 296) might mean _____

    _____

6. **Fortnight** (p. 296) might mean _____

    _____

7. **Comrades** (p. 296) might mean _____

    _____

8. **Ecstatic** (p. 297) might mean _____

    _____

Let's see how you did. Check your answers, write the exact definitions, and reread the sentence in *Eclipse* where each word appears. Then complete the drills on the next page.

1. **Appalled** (p. 287) means *horrified*. The context defines the word: in preceding sentences Bella "gasped," "breathed in horror," and "gaped."

2. **Anonymity** (p. 289) means *not being identified*. Interestingly, *a-* means *without*, and *nym-* or *nom-* refers to *name*, as in *pseudonym* (a fake or pen name), so *anonymity* means *without name—not being identified*.

3. **Proportions** (p. 290) means *parts of the whole*. I feel a math lesson coming on, maybe some cross-multiplying . . . . Well, I will just leave it with this: *proportions* sounds like *portions* (parts), and means *parts of the whole*.

4. **Circumspectly** (p. 292) means *carefully* and was a synonym for *vigilant* (watchful) in Group 20. Remember that *circumspect* translates as *looking around—watchful and careful*. The other synonym was *wary*.

5. **Wane** (p. 296) means *decrease*. A fancy word for the opposite of *wane* is *wax*.

6. **Fortnight** (p. 296) means *two-week period*. When I first learned this word I thought it must be military and have to do with nights in a fort, but it's actually just short for ***fourteen nights***, which is two weeks. In the United States, this word is rarely used (except sometimes on the SAT, ACT, GED, or SSAT!), but in your pal Robert Pattinson's homeland, England, the word is more common. Now that you know the word, too, you are even more perfectly matched! ☺

7. **Comrades** (p. 296) means *companions,* and "comrades in arms" means *fellow soldiers*.

8. **Ecstatic** (p. 297) means *thrilled* and was a synonym for *exuberant* in Group 13. The other synonyms were *buoyant, ebullient, elated, euphoric, exultant, jubilant,* and *rapturous*.

Drills

Synonyms: Select the word or phrase whose meaning is closest to the word in capital letters.

1. CIRCUMSPECT
   A. anonymous
   B. appalled
   C. ebullient
   D. buoyant
   E. wary

2. WANE
   A. conceal
   B. decrease
   C. reconcile
   D. connote
   E. covet

3. FORTNIGHT
   A. two weeks
   B. comrade
   C. proportion
   D. modus operandi
   E. paroxysm

4. ECSTATIC
   A. gregarious
   B. dexterous
   C. elated
   D. adept
   E. adroit

Analogies: Select the answer choice that best completes the meaning of the sentence.

5. Wane is to wax as
   A. covet is to escalate
   B. pacify is to amplify
   C. decrease is to intercede
   D. reduce is to augment
   E. choreograph is to encroach

6. Appalled is to gasp as
   A. anonymous is to scold
   B. vigilant is to bow
   C. slovenly is to aspire
   D. amenable is to nod
   E. cordial is to jibe

Sentence Completions: Choose the word that, when inserted in the sentence, *best* fits the meaning of the sentence as a whole.

7. The dancers whirled and twirled to the driving beat until the room was filled with a bursting _____ energy.
   A. heterogeneous
   B. manifold
   C. ecstatic
   D. multifarious
   E. transitory

8. Peeta was _____ by the lack of humanity and the brutality of the games.
   A. alleviated
   B. assuaged
   C. mollified
   D. placated
   E. appalled

1. **E.** *Circumspect* and *wary* mean *cautious. Anonymous* means *unnamed,* appalled means *horrified,* and *ebullient* and *buoyant* mean *thrilled. Buoyant* comes from a buoy that floats in the ocean and means *floating on air—thrilled.*

2. **B.** *Wane* means *decrease. Conceal* means *hide, reconcile* means *settle, connote* means *imply,* and *covet* means *want.*

3. **A.** *Fortnight* means *two weeks. Comrade* means *companion, proportion* means *part of the whole, modus operandi* means *way of doing,* and *paroxysm* means *attack of emotion.*

4. **C.** *Ecstatic* and *elated* both mean *thrilled. Gregarious* means *friendly,* and *dexterous, adept,* and *adroit* mean *graceful and skilled.*

5. **D.** "Wane (decrease) is the opposite of wax (increase)."
   - A. Covet (want) is the opposite of escalate (increase) . . . no.
   - B. Pacify (soothe) is the opposite of amplify (increase) . . . maybe.
   - C. Decrease is the opposite of intercede (intervene) . . . no.
   - (D.) Reduce is the opposite of augment (increase) . . . yes!
   - E. Choreograph (plan out) is the opposite of encroach (intrude) . . . no.

   Choice D is best. Soothe can be the opposite of increase, but not necessarily, whereas reduce is definitely the opposite of increase.

6. **D.** "An appalled (horrified) person might gasp."
   - A. An anonymous (unnamed) person might scold . . . no, not necessarily.
   - B. A vigilant (watchful) person might bow . . . no, not necessarily.
   - C. A slovenly (messy) person might aspire . . . no, not necessarily.
   - (D.) An amenable (agreeable) person might nod . . . yes.
   - E. A cordial (friendly) person might jibe (taunt) . . . no.

7. **C.** "The dancers whirled and twirled to the driving beat until the room was filled with a bursting *energetic/whirling* energy."

   If you can't come up with a word for the blank, use the process of elimination. Especially in this case, it's critical to eliminate choices **only** when you are absolutely positive that they don't fit. Then choose the best of the remaining choices. *Ecstatic* means *thrilled* and fits the evidence of the sentence best.

8. **E.** "Peeta was *upset* by the lack of humanity and the brutality of the games."

   Appalled means *horrified.*

Unassailable Logic?

Find each of the following words on the *Eclipse* page number provided.
Based on the way each word is used in the book, guess at its definition.

1. **Purge** (p. 298) might mean _____
   _____

2. **Tenuous** (p. 299) might mean _____
   _____

3. **Nomads** (p. 303) might mean _____
   _____

4. **Omniscience** (p. 305) might mean _____
   _____

5. **Innate** (p. 306) might mean _____
   _____

6. **Commemorate** (p. 311) might mean _____
   _____

7. **Elimination** (p. 312) might mean _____
   _____

8. **Unassailable** (p. 313) might mean _____
   _____

Let's see how you did. Check your answers, write the exact definitions, and reread the sentence in *Eclipse* where each word appears. Then complete the drills on the next page.

1. **Purge** (p. 298) means *get rid of something* or *cleanse.* This is described two sentences later: *"dispose of them."*

2. **Tenuous** (p. 299) means *weak.* Jasper describes the word right after he says it: *"easily broken."*

3. **Nomads** (p. 303) means *wanderers.* Synonyms: itinerants, transients. Remember that the word *transient* was a synonym in Group 22 for *transitory,* meaning *temporary.* That makes sense since a *transient* (nomad, wanderer) moves around and is always a *transitory* (temporary) visitor.

4. **Omniscience** (p. 305) means *the state of knowing everything.* Remember from Group 8 that *omni-* means *all,* as in *omnipresent* (present all over). *Scient-* refers to *knowing,* as in *science* (the gathering of knowledge), so *omniscience* means *all-knowingness—the state of knowing everything.* With Alice and Edward by his side, Aro would be able to read all thoughts (by touching Edward) and see the future (by touching Alice); he would *know everything.* Greedy Aro!

5. **Innate** (p. 306) means *inborn.* "Carlisle's innate calm" means that, for Carlisle, being calm is a core quality—it comes naturally and is part of who he is. Synonyms: inherent, intrinsic.

6. **Commemorate** (p. 311) means *honor and celebrate;* Alice loves to plan a party! *Commemorate* breaks down to *com-* (together) and *memor* (as in *remember*), so *commemorate* means *remember together— honor and celebrate.*

7. **Elimination** (p. 312) means *removal,* like when Danny Gokey was **eliminated** from *American Idol* after singing Joe Cocker's "You Are So Beautiful." *Elimination* can also mean *killing,* and that's how Alice meant it here in *Eclipse.*

8. **Unassailable** (p. 313) means *not attackable* or *definite.* Synonyms: impregnable, incontrovertible, indisputable, indubitable, invincible, inviolable, invulnerable, irrefutable, manifest, patent, unconquerable.

Synonyms: Select the word or phrase whose meaning is closest to the word in capital letters.

1. PURGE
   A. commemorate
   B. prophesize
   C. unequivocal
   D. refute
   E. cleanse

2. TENUOUS
   A. nomadic
   B. omnipresent
   C. inherent
   D. weak
   E. intrinsic

3. OMNISCIENT
   A. all-knowing
   B. unassailable
   C. impregnable
   D. inviolable
   E. patent

4. INNATE
   A. indisputable
   B. inherent
   C. invulnerable
   D. invincible
   E. irrefutable

Analogies: Select the answer choice that best completes the meaning of the sentence.

5. Dirge is to commemorates as
   A. lament is to transmutes
   B. soiree is to goads
   C. requiem is to honors
   D. threnody is to augments
   E. rampage is to polarizes

6. Nomad is to transitory as
   A. traveler is to eliminated
   B. comrade is to rapturous
   C. pessimist is to prolific
   D. wanderer is to venerated
   E. itinerant is to impermanent

Sentence Completions: Choose the word that, when inserted in the sentence, *best* fits the meaning of the sentence as a whole.

7. Francis backed up her claims with solid evidence and presented a(n) _____ case when defending her thesis.
   A. tenuous
   B. omniscient
   C. innate
   D. unassailable
   E. vulnerable

8. Originally the Comanche were a(n) _____ group who hunted and gathered throughout what is now New Mexico and the surrounding areas.
   A. invulnerable
   B. eliminated
   C. nomadic
   D. omnipresent
   E. enigmatic

1. **E.** *Purge* means *cleanse. Commemorate* means *remember and honor, prophesize* means *predict, unequivocal* means *definite,* and *refute* means *disprove.* You learned that *irrefutable* means *not attackable* or *definite,* which makes sense since *ir-* means *not,* so *irrefutable* means *not disprovable—definite.*

2. **D.** *Tenuous* means *weak.* Use the process of elimination; only choice D is close. *Nomadic* means *wandering, omnipresent* means *all-present,* and *inherent* and *intrinsic* mean *inborn.*

3. **A.** *Omniscient* means *all-knowing. Unassailable, impregnable, inviolable,* and *patent* mean *not attackable* or *definite.*

4. **B.** *Innate* and *inherent* mean *inborn. Indisputable, invulnerable, invincible,* and *irrefutable* mean *not attackable* or *definite.*

5. **C.** "A dirge (expression of mourning) commemorates a dead person."
   A. A lament (expression of mourning) transmutes (changes) a dead person . . . no.
   B. A soiree (evening party) goads (urges) a dead person . . . no.
   C. A requiem (expression of mourning) honors a dead person . . . yes!
   D. A threnody (expression of mourning) augments (increases) a dead person . . . no.
   E. A rampage (out-of-control behavior) polarizes (clearly divides) a dead person . . . no.

6. **E.** "A nomad's (wanderer's) home is transitory (temporary)."
   A. A traveler's home is eliminated . . . no.
   B. A comrade's (companion's) home is rapturous (excited) . . . no.
   C. A pessimist's (someone expecting bad things to happen) home is prolific (abundant) . . . no.
   D. A wanderer's home is venerated (respected) . . . no, not necessarily.
   E. An itinerant's (wanderer's) home is impermanent (temporary) . . . yes.

7. **D.** "Francis backed up her claims with solid evidence and presented a(n) *solid* case when defending her thesis."
   Unassailable means *not attackable* or *definite* and is the best answer.

8. **C.** "Originally the Comanche were a(n) *????* group who hunted and gathered throughout what is now New Mexico and the surrounding areas."
   Nomadic means *wandering* and fits best. Use evidence in the sentence to choose your answer. You know that the Comanche "hunted and gathered throughout what is now New Mexico and the surrounding areas," so *nomadic* makes sense. They may have been *invulnerable, eliminated, omnipresent,* or even *enigmatic,* but you only have evidence in the sentence that they were *nomadic.*

Quiz 5

I. Let's review some of the words that you've seen in Groups 21–25. Match each of the following words to the correct definition or synonym on the right. Then check the solutions on page 172.

1. Adulation	A. Slow to comprehend
2. Abstraction	B. Threnody
3. Obtuse	C. Prediction
4. Transitory	D. Wary
5. Dirge	E. Veneration
6. Prolific	F. Conceptual
7. Diverse	G. Evanescent
8. Conflagration	H. Euphoric
9. Prophecy	I. Weak
10. Circumspect	J. All-knowing
11. Wane	K. Widespread
12. Ecstatic	L. Itinerant
13. Tenuous	M. Decrease
14. Nomad	N. Motley
15. Omniscient	O. Fire

II. Let's review several of the word parts that you've seen in Groups 21–25. Match each of the following word parts to the correct definition or synonym on the right. Then check the solutions on page 172.

16. Re-	A. Beyond
17. Para-	B. With
18. Carn-	C. Without
19. -Cide	D. Again
20. Con-	E. Killing
21. A-	F. Flesh

Group 26

Incorrigible Behavior

Find each of the following words on the *Eclipse* page number provided. Based on the way each word is used in the book, guess at its definition.

1. **Generic** (p. 315) might mean _____

   _____

2. **Superficial** (p. 315) might mean _____

   _____

3. **Extricated** (p. 315) might mean _____

   _____

4. **Custodial** (p. 318) might mean _____

   _____

5. **Haggard** (p. 322) might mean _____

   _____

6. **Glutton** (p. 329) might mean _____

   _____

7. **Incorrigible** (p. 339) might mean _____

   _____

8. **Percolating** (p. 344) might mean _____

   _____

Let's see how you did. Check your answers, write the exact definitions, and reread the sentence in *Eclipse* where each word appears. Then complete the drills on the next page.

1. **Generic** (p. 315) sounds like *general* and means *common, not special,* or *nonspecific,* such as the **generic** oats that you might buy for breakfast instead of the Quaker brand of oatmeal.

2. **Superficial** (p. 315) means *shallow* or *on the surface.* This is a great word to break apart. *Super-* means *above* or *beyond,* as in *Superman* (**beyond** man) and the high-level word *supercilious* (acting **beyond** or **superior** to others—*arrogant*). *Ficial* implies *face,* so *superficial* means *above the face of something—shallow,* rather than deep.

3. **Extricated** (p. 315) means *freed.* Remember that *ex-* means *out*—Edward took himself **out** of Bella's embrace. Synonym: disentangled. I like this synonym because it gives a great image of Bella and Edward's arms and legs intertwined (tangled) in an embrace.

4. **Custodial** (p. 318) means *relating to protective or parental care.* Specifically, *custodial guardians* refers to the guardians appointed to a child by a court. Do you think Edward and Jacob are like **custodial guardians** to Bella? That's a pretty weird image!

5. **Haggard** (p. 322) means *looking exhausted and unwell.*

6. **Glutton** (p. 329) means *a person greedy or overeager for something.* In *Eclipse,* the phrase "a glutton for punishment" means *a person who is greedy or eager for something that will be unpleasant.* Interestingly, *glutton* can also refer to a *wolverine,* which is *a wolf-like animal with a shaggy dark coat and a bushy tail!*

7. **Incorrigible** (p. 339) means *unapologetic and unlikely to change.* Synonyms: impenitent, inveterate, irredeemable, remorseless.

8. **Percolating** (p. 344) means *bubbling* or *spreading.* Years ago, before Starbucks made French presses (a type of coffee maker) all the rage, people brewed coffee at home in a pot called a *percolator,* and many percolators had a part of the lid where you could see the coffee **bubbling** as it brewed.

Synonyms: Select the word or phrase whose meaning is closest to the word in capital letters.

1. EXTRICATED
   A. freed
   B. generic
   C. superficial
   D. supercilious
   E. percolating

2. HAGGARD
   A. custodial
   B. incorrigible
   C. impenitent
   D. inveterate
   E. exhausted

3. GLUTTON
   A. unapologetic person
   B. greedy person
   C. tired person
   D. free person
   E. bubbly person

4. INCORRIGIBLE
   A. superficial
   B. inveterate
   C. intertwined
   D. generic
   E. custodial

Analogies: Select the answer choice that best completes the meaning of the sentence.

5. Superficial is to deep as
   A. supercilious is to unassailable
   B. extricated is to innate
   C. haggard is to robust
   D. incorrigible is to nomadic
   E. tenuous is to omniscient

6. Incorrigible is to remorseless as
   A. manifest is to eliminated
   B. circumspect is to ecstatic
   C. inherent is to intrinsic
   D. diverse is to indisputable
   E. motley is to pessimistic

Sentence Completions: Choose the word that, when inserted in the sentence, *best* fits the meaning of the sentence as a whole.

7. Ideas began percolating in Larry's mind when he saw the _____ look on Rich's face; he knew that Rich was tired.
   A. generic
   B. superficial
   C. custodial
   D. haggard
   E. impenitent

8. The guest speaker at the convention was _____; he offended the audience repeatedly and refused to apologize for his intemperate remarks.
   A. purging
   B. omnipresent
   C. inviolable
   D. patent
   E. incorrigible

1. **A.** *Extricated* means *freed. Generic* means *general, superficial* means *shallow, supercilious* means *arrogant,* and *percolating* means *bubbling.*

2. **E.** *Haggard* means *exhausted looking,* so choice E is best. *Custodial* means *relating to protective or parental care,* and *incorrigible, impenitent,* and *inveterate* mean *unapologetic and unlikely to change.*

3. **B.** *Glutton* means *greedy person.* As always, use the process of elimination to find the closest answer—cross off answers that you are **sure** don't work and choose the best of what's left.

4. **B.** *Incorrigible* and *inveterate* mean *unapologetic and unlikely to change. Superficial* means *shallow, intertwined* means *entangled, generic* means *general,* and *custodial* means *relating to protective or parental care.*

5. **C.** "Superficial (shallow) is the opposite of deep."
   A. Supercilious (arrogant) is the opposite of unassailable (not attackable) . . . no.
   B. Extricated (removed) is the opposite of innate (inborn) . . . no.
   C. Haggard (unhealthy-looking) is the opposite of robust (healthy) . . . maybe.
   D. Incorrigible (unapologetic) is the opposite of nomadic (wandering) . . . no.
   E. Tenuous (weak) is the opposite of omniscient (all-knowing) . . . maybe.
   Choice C is best. *Tenuous* (weak) is not necessarily the opposite of *all-knowing.* If someone is all-knowing, they may therefore be strong, but not necessarily. The correct answer should be clearly and directly related.

6. **C.** "Incorrigible means remorseless."
   A. Manifest (definite) means eliminated (removed) . . . no.
   B. Circumspect (wary) means ecstatic (thrilled) . . . no.
   C. Inherent (inborn) means intrinsic (inborn) . . . yes!
   D. Diverse means indisputable (definite) . . . no.
   E. Motley (diverse) means pessimistic (expecting bad things) . . . no.

7. **D.** "Ideas began percolating in Larry's mind when he saw the <u>tired</u> look on Rich's face; he knew that Rich was tired."
   Haggard means *exhausted* and fits best.

8. **E.** "The guest speaker at the convention was <u>offensive</u>; he offended the audience repeatedly and refused to apologize for his intemperate remarks."
   Incorrigible means *unapologetic* and fits best. If you don't know a word in the sentence, such as *intemperate* (excessive), don't give up. Vibe the word out or even ignore it and try anyway. Most standardized test sentences are designed so that you don't need to know the definition of every word!

Group 27

Pandemonium

Find each of the following words on the *Eclipse* page number provided. Based on the way each word is used in the book, guess at its definition.

1. **Epoch** (p. 346) might mean _____

   _____

2. **Sophisticated** (p. 350) might mean _____

   _____

3. **Pandemonium** (p. 352) might mean _____

   _____

4. **Valedictorian** (p. 354) might mean _____

   _____

5. **Trite** (p. 354) might mean _____

   _____

6. **Farce** (p. 354) might mean _____

   _____

7. **Beseeching** (p. 359) might mean _____

   _____

8. **Morosely** (p. 360) might mean _____

   _____

Let's see how you did. Check your answers, write the exact definitions, and reread the sentence in *Eclipse* where each word appears. Then complete the drills on the next page.

1. **Epoch** (p. 346) means *period of history.* I don't usually use words directly from chapter titles, but this is a great review of *era* from Group 17. The other synonym was *eon.* Here's a question from your dream English class: Why is this chapter called "Epoch"? Discuss the answer with your friends.

2. **Sophisticated** (p. 350) means *advanced, complex, mature,* or *fashionable.* The Cullens are **sophisticated.** In Group 18, you learned the words *naïve, juvenile, puerile,* and *sophomoric* that mean *immature,* the opposite of *sophisticated.* Know anyone like that? Oh, that was cold. Sorry, Jake.

3. **Pandemonium** (p. 352) means *chaos. Pandemonium* contains *pan-,* meaning *all,* as in *pandemic* from Group 19. So *pan**demon**ium* means **all** *the* **demons** *come out*—chaos. Synonyms: anarchy, bedlam, havoc, mayhem, rumpus, tumult, turmoil. I love that I get to use the word *rumpus* here, like in *Where the Wild Things Are* when Max is crowned King of the Wild Things and proclaims, "Let the wild rumpus start!"

4. **Valedictorian** (p. 354) means *highest-ranked student in the class* and comes from the Latin for *saying goodbye,* since the valedictorian usually gives the final speech at graduation. *Dict-* means *to say,* and helps you remember words like *diction* (one's style of speaking or writing) and *dictum* (proclamation).

5. **Trite** (p. 354) means *overused* and was a synonym for *hokey* in Group 1. The other synonyms were *banal* (overused and boring), *cliché, hackneyed,* and *platitudinous.*

6. **Farce** (p. 354) means *sham* or *lie.* Synonyms: charade, pretense.

7. **Beseeching** (p. 359) means *begging.* Synonyms: entreating, imploring, importuning.

8. **Morosely** (p. 360) means *gloomily,* just like the "depressed-looking stuffed elk" on the wall at the Lodge.

Synonyms: Select the word or phrase whose meaning is closest to the word in capital letters.

1. EPOCH
   A. farce
   B. glutton
   C. fortnight
   D. eon
   E. comrade

2. PANDEMONIUM
   A. conflagration
   B. rumpus
   C. concealment
   D. prophecy
   E. methodology

3. TRITE
   A. arduous
   B. Herculean
   C. prolific
   D. ephemeral
   E. hackneyed

4. BESEECH
   A. entreat
   B. extricate
   C. percolate
   D. purge
   E. commemorate

Analogies: Select the answer choice that best completes the meaning of the sentence.

5. Sophisticated is to puerile as
   A. advanced is to platitudinous
   B. haggard is to evanescent
   C. hokey is to naïve
   D. fashionable is to cliché
   E. mature is to sophomoric

6. Morose is to ecstatic as
   A. farce is to charade
   B. lie is to pretense
   C. implore is to importune
   D. diction is to dictum
   E. anarchy is to order

Sentence Completions: Choose the word that, when inserted in the sentence, *best* fits the meaning of the sentence as a whole.

7. Once she found out that she was valedictorian, Chloe _____ the principal to let her rap her graduation speech with her best friends singing backup.
   A. implored
   B. loathed
   C. placated
   D. imprinted
   E. reproved

8. The advisor of the school paper warned students against using _____ expressions that lessen the impact of their writing.
   A. morose
   B. beseeching
   C. tumultuous
   D. trite
   E. omniscient

1. **D.** *Epoch* and *eon* mean *period of time in history. Farce* means *sham, glutton* means *greedy person, fortnight* means *two-week period,* and *comrade* means *companion. Fortnight* is the second best answer, but *epoch* and *eon* imply a **long** period of time in history.

2. **B.** *Pandemonium* and *rumpus* mean *disorder. Conflagration* means *fire, concealment* means *hiding, prophecy* means *prediction,* and *methodology* means *way of doing something.*

3. **E.** *Trite* and *hackneyed* mean *overused. Arduous* and *Herculean* mean *difficult* or *requiring great strength. Prolific* means *abundant,* and *ephemeral* means *fleeting.*

4. **A.** *Beseech* and *entreat* mean *beg. Extricate* means *remove, percolate* means *bubble, purge* means *cleanse,* and *commemorate* means *honor and celebrate.*

5. **E.** "Sophisticated (mature) is the opposite of puerile (immature)."
   A. Advanced is the opposite of platitudinous (overused) . . . no.
   B. Haggard (exhausted looking) is the opposite of evanescent (fleeting) . . . no.
   C. Hokey (overused) is the opposite of naïve (immature) . . . no.
   D. Fashionable is the opposite of cliché (overused) . . . maybe.
   E. Mature is the opposite of sophomoric (immature) . . . yes!
   Choice E is a more clear and direct answer than choice D—something that is fashionable may or may not be overused.

6. **E.** "Morose (gloomy) is the opposite of ecstatic (thrilled)."
   A. Farce (sham) is the opposite of charade (sham) . . . no.
   B. Lie is the opposite of pretense (sham) . . . no.
   C. Implore (beg) is the opposite of importune (beg) . . . no.
   D. Diction (way of speaking) is the opposite of dictum (proclamation) . . . no.
   E. Anarchy (disorder) is the opposite of order . . . yes!

7. **A.** "Once she found out that she was valedictorian, Chloe *asked* the principal to let her rap her graduation speech with her best friends singing backup."
   Implored means *begged.* Chloe may have *loathed* or *placated* the principal, and for all you know she may have *imprinted* or *reproved* him, but you have evidence **only** that she was asking him "to let her rap . . . ", so choice A fits best. Base your answer on the info directly stated in the sentence.

8. **D.** "The advisor of the school paper warned students against using *weak* expressions that lessen the impact of their writing."
   Trite means *overused* and fits best. That is certainly the best answer using the process of elimination. *Morose* means *gloomy, beseeching* means *begging, tumultuous* means *chaotic,* and *omniscient* means *all-knowing.*

Desperation

Find each of the following words on the *Eclipse* page number provided. Based on the way each word is used in the book, guess at its definition.

1. **Impromptu** (p. 361) might mean _____

   _____

2. **Reclusive** (p. 367) might mean _____

   _____

3. **Epiphany** (p. 367) might mean _____

   _____

4. **Desperation** (p. 367) might mean _____

   _____

5. **Rescinded** (p. 371) might mean _____

   _____

6. **Crypt** (p. 371) might mean _____

   _____

7. **Boisterously** (p. 383) might mean _____

   _____

8. **Euphoric** (p. 383) might mean _____

   _____

116 Let's see how you did. Check your answers, write the exact definitions, and reread the sentence in *Eclipse* where each word appears. Then complete the drills on the next page.

Definitions

1. **Impromptu** (p. 361) means *spontaneous*.

2. **Reclusive** (p. 367) is the opposite of *gregarious* (friendly, social) and means *solitary*. The Cullens have been much less **reclusive** since Bella showed up; they even share a lunch table with Angela, Ben, and Eric! A *hermit* (*solitary person*—like Bella when Edward left in *New Moon*) is *reclusive*.

3. **Epiphany** (p. 367) means *sudden insight,* like the name of T-Pain's 2007 album.

4. **Desperation** (p. 367) sounds like *desperate* and means *distress and lack of hope*.

5. **Rescinded** (p. 371) means *taken back*. Synonyms: nullified, revoked.

6. **Crypt** (p. 371) means *tomb,* like when Xander says to Buffy, "Or better yet, why don't you just go sit on top of a crypt and flaunt your neck cleavage until Dracula shows up. Then you two can talk in private." (The WB, *Buffy the Vampire Slayer,* "Buffy vs. Dracula," 1997) Synonyms: ossuary, sepulcher.

7. **Boisterously** (p. 383) means *with exuberance*. Remember the word *exuberance* (excitement) from Group 13? Emmett is usually pretty exuberant, especially when there's a fight coming.

8. **Euphoric** (p. 383) means *thrilled* and was a synonym for *ecstatic* in Group 24. The other synonyms were *buoyant, ebullient, elated, euphoric, exultant, jubilant,* and *rapturous*.

Synonyms: Select the word or phrase whose meaning is closest to the word in capital letters.

1. RECLUSIVE
   A. gregarious
   B. buoyant
   C. ebullient
   D. solitary
   E. jubilant

2. EPIPHANY
   A. sudden insight
   B. crypt
   C. ossuary
   D. sepulcher
   E. valedictorian

3. BOISTEROUS
   A. impromptu
   B. exuberant
   C. puerile
   D. sophomoric
   E. supercilious

4. EUPHORIC
   A. surly
   B. churlish
   C. petulant
   D. stringent
   E. elated

Analogies: Select the answer choice that best completes the meaning of the sentence.

5. Desperation is to hope as
   A. ebullience is to heterogeneity
   B. elation is to anonymity
   C. mayhem is to anarchy
   D. reclusiveness is to gregariousness
   E. bedlam is to chaos

6. Hermit is to reclusive as
   A. vampire is to unchaste
   B. Volturi is to scarlet
   C. werewolf is to boisterous
   D. choreographer is to impromptu
   E. zombie is to haggard

Sentence Completions: Choose the word that, when inserted in the sentence, *best* fits the meaning of the sentence as a whole.

7. Normally boisterous and energetic, her mood changed to _____ as she entered the haunted crypt.
   A. euphoria
   B. obtuse
   C. adulation
   D. desperation
   E. variegated

8. Eudora's epiphany showed her the mistake in her plan to _____ her bid on the property, and so she let her offer remain.
   A. rescind
   B. beseech
   C. entreat
   D. extricate
   E. reconcile

Solutions

1. **D.** *Reclusive* means *solitary*. *Gregarious* means *friendly*, and *buoyant*, *ebullient*, and *jubilant* mean *excited*.

2. **A.** *Epiphany* means *sudden insight*. *Crypt, ossuary*, and *sepulcher* mean *tomb*. *Valedictorian* means *student ranked first in a class*.

3. **B.** *Boisterous* and *exuberant* mean *excited*. *Impromptu* means *spontaneous*, *puerile* and *sophomoric* mean *immature*, and *supercilious* means *arrogant*.

4. **E.** *Euphoric* and *elated* mean *thrilled*. *Surly* and *churlish* mean *rude and unfriendly*. *Petulant* means *irritable*, and *stringent* means *strict*.

5. **D.** "Desperation (distress, lack of hope) is the absence of hope."
   A. Ebullience (excitement) is the absence of heterogeneity (diversity) . . . no.
   B. Elation (excitement) is the absence of anonymity (lack of being named) . . . no.
   C. Mayhem (chaos) is the absence of anarchy (chaos) . . . no.
   D. Reclusiveness (solitariness) is the absence of gregariousness (socialness) . . . yes.
   E. Bedlam (chaos) is the absence of chaos . . . no.
   Using the process of elimination, choice D is best.

6. **E.** "A hermit is a reclusive (solitary) person."
   A. A vampire is an unchaste (sexually liberal) person . . . whoa now, that depends on the vampire!
   B. A Volturi is a scarlet (bright red) person . . . no, just their eyes, and only when fed!
   C. A werewolf is a boisterous (energetic) person . . . maybe the young ones, but Sam Uley is fairly mellow.
   D. A choreographer is an impromptu (spontaneous) person . . . maybe, but a choreographer probably plans the dance steps in advance.
   E. A zombie is a haggard (unhealthy-looking) person . . . yes, zombies look pretty unhealthy; they are dead after all.

7. **D.** "Normally boisterous and energetic, her mood changed to _not boisterous and energetic_ as she entered the haunted crypt."
   Desperation means *distress* and *lack of hope* and fits best.

8. **A.** "Eudora's epiphany showed her the mistake in her plan to _not remain_ her bid on the property, and so she let her offer remain."
   Rescind means *take back*.

Errant Thoughts

Find each of the following words on the *Eclipse* page number provided. Based on the way each word is used in the book, guess at its definition.

1. **Implacable** (p. 387) might mean _____

   _____

2. **Havoc** (p. 389) might mean _____

   _____

3. **Reproach** (p. 396) might mean _____

   _____

4. **Gangly** (p. 399) might mean _____

   _____

5. **Exuding** (p. 399) might mean _____

   _____

6. **Errant** (p. 407) might mean _____

   _____

7. **Ludicrous** (p. 413) might mean _____

   _____

8. **Injunction** (p. 415) might mean _____

   _____

120 Let's see how you did. Check your answers, write the exact definitions, and reread the sentence in *Eclipse* where each word appears. Then complete the drills on the next page.

Definitions

1. **Implacable** (p. 387) means *unstoppable* or *unable to be satisfied*. This actually comes from the word *placate,* meaning *satisfy* or *soothe,* a synonym for *appease* in Group 5. Since *im-* means *not, implacable* means *not satisfiable.* You can see this in the context; Bella describes Victoria as "a force of nature . . . unavoidable . . . . " Synonyms: inexorable, intransigent, relentless, unappeasable.

2. **Havoc** (p. 389) means *disorder or destruction*. This could be a synonym for *pandemonium* from Group 27. The other synonyms were *anarchy, bedlam, mayhem, rumpus, tumult,* and *turmoil*. This paragraph in *Eclipse* is where you discover Victoria's supernatural vampire gift for avoiding capture.

3. **Reproach** (p. 396) means *scolding* and was a synonym for *reproof* in Group 18. The other synonyms were *admonishment, censure, rebuke,* and *reprimand*.

4. **Gangly** (p. 399) means *tall, skinny,* and *awkward*. The word *gangly* even sounds awkward and is described in the context in *Eclipse* as "uncoordinated." Synonym: lanky. *Eclipse* quiz: Who is this new gangly wolf? Discuss the answer with your friends.

5. **Exuding** (p. 399) means *giving off* or *radiating*.

6. **Errant** (p. 407) means *stray* and comes from the word *err,* meaning *make a mistake*. So Jasper's *errant* thought was a **mistake**—his thoughts had **strayed.** I don't think Jasper really considered his idea to be errant, but he was afraid of Edward's reaction.

7. **Ludicrous** (p. 413) means *unreasonable or ridiculous;* no disrespect to rapper and philanthropist Christopher Brian Bridges, a.k.a. Ludacris.

8. **Injunction** (p. 415) means *formal order*. Seth can't ignore **formal orders** from the Alpha. Synonyms: decree, dictum, directive, edict, fiat, mandate, proclamation, writ.

Synonyms: Select the word or phrase whose meaning is closest to the word in capital letters.

1. IMPLACABLE
   A. inexorable
   B. errant
   C. ludicrous
   D. impromptu
   E. reclusive

2. HAVOC
   A. desperation
   B. disconsolation
   C. exuberance
   D. euphoria
   E. mayhem

3. REPROACH
   A. rescind
   B. reproof
   C. reuse
   D. retire
   E. refer

4. GANGLY
   A. exuding
   B. deft
   C. lanky
   D. dexterous
   E. adroit

Analogies: Select the answer choice that best completes the meaning of the sentence.

5. Implacable is to intransigent as
   A. inexorable is to gregarious
   B. relentless is to reclusive
   C. unappeasable is to reproachful
   D. gangly is to hefty
   E. errant is to stray

6. Tornado is to havoc as
   A. nomad is to omniscience
   B. injunction is to epiphany
   C. Cullen is to euphoria
   D. newborn vampire is to carnage
   E. rampage is to abstraction

Sentence Completions: Choose the word that, when inserted in the sentence, *best* fits the meaning of the sentence as a whole.

7. The prank was so _____ and contrived that no one believed it even for a second.
   A. gangly
   B. lanky
   C. reproachful
   D. boisterous
   E. ludicrous

8. Mina ordered Jennifer to go home, but Jennifer ignored this _____ and stayed by Mina's side.
   A. exuding
   B. bedlam
   C. directive
   D. epiphany
   E. elation

1. **A.** *Implacable* and *inexorable* mean *unstoppable*. *Errant* means *stray*, *ludicrous* means *ridiculous*, *impromptu* means *spontaneous*, and *reclusive* means *solitary*.

2. **E.** *Havoc* and *mayhem* mean *chaos*. *Desperation* and *disconsolation* mean *distress and lack of hope*, and *exuberance* and *euphoria* mean *excitement*.

3. **B.** *Reproach* and *reproof* mean *scold*. *Rescind* means *take back*.

4. **C.** *Gangly* and *lanky* mean *tall, thin, and awkward*. Use the process of elimination. *Exuding* means *radiating*, and *deft, dexterous,* and *adroit* mean *skilled and graceful*.

5. **E.** "Implacable (unsatisfiable) is similar to intransigent (stubborn)."
   A. Inexorable (unstoppable) is similar to gregarious (social) . . . no.
   B. Relentless (unstoppable) is similar to reclusive (solitary) . . . no.
   C. Unappeasable (unsatisfiable) is similar to reproachful (scolding) . . . no.
   D. Gangly (tall, thin, and awkward) is similar to hefty (large) . . . no.
   (E.) Errant (stray) is similar to stray . . . yes.

6. **D.** "A tornado causes havoc (disorder)."
   A. A nomad (wanderer) causes omniscience (all-knowingness) . . . no.
   B. An injunction (formal order) causes an epiphany (insight) . . . no.
   C. A Cullen causes euphoria (bliss) . . . maybe, but it depends on which Cullen.
   (D.) A newborn vampire causes carnage . . . yes, well, with one exception, but you won't find out about that 'til *Breaking Dawn*.
   E. A rampage (out-of-control behavior) causes abstraction (distracted thinking) . . . no, not necessarily.

7. **E.** "The prank was so *contrived* and contrived that no one believed it even for a second."
   Use the process of elimination. *Ludicrous* means *ridiculous*, and is the best answer. *Contrived* means *fake*, but you could get this question correct from the words "no one believed it for a second" even if you didn't know that definition of *contrived*!

8. **C.** "Mina ordered Jennifer to go home, but Jennifer ignored this *order* and stayed by Mina's side."
   Directive sounds like *direction* and means *formal order*.

Group 30
Ramifications

Find each of the following words on the *Eclipse* page number provided. Based on the way each word is used in the book, guess at its definition.

1. **Plural** (p. 416) might mean _____

   _____

2. **Anguish** (p. 435) might mean _____

   _____

3. **Ramifications** (p. 436) might mean _____

   _____

4. **Deprecatingly** (p. 438) might mean _____

   _____

5. **Ruefully** (p. 439) might mean _____

   _____

6. **Matrimony** (p. 440) might mean _____

   _____

7. **Bleak** (p. 445) might mean _____

   _____

8. **Inept** (p. 445) might mean _____

   _____

Let's see how you did. Check your answers, write the exact definitions, and reread the sentence in *Eclipse* where each word appears. Then complete the drills on the next page.

1. **Plural** (p. 416) means *more than one. Wolf* is singular (one); *wolves* is plural.

2. **Anguish** (p. 435) means *suffering.*

3. **Ramifications** (p. 436) means *negative effects.* This is one of those impressive vocabulary words that you can add to almost any standardized test essay to gain points. For example, "The ramifications of Bella's choosing Edward over Jacob are . . . " Use this word correctly in your essay and you'll gain points; I guarantee it!

4. **Deprecatingly** (p. 438) means *in a belittling or criticizing way.* Edward is **belittling** the enormous diamond that he just gave Bella, pretending it is only a meaningless "bauble" and "not a big deal" so that she'll accept it. Synonyms: denigratingly, disparagingly, pejoratively.

5. **Ruefully** (p. 439) means *regretfully.*

6. **Matrimony** (p. 440) means *marriage.*

7. **Bleak** (p. 445) means *gloomy.* It can also mean *not hopeful,* though I think that Edward was more **gloomy** than **not hopeful.** There may be a line of hopefuls waiting to date Bella, but even without reading her thoughts, he must know that no one else stands a chance with her, right?

8. **Inept** (p. 445) means *clumsy and unskilled.* Here's an awesome synonym: maladroit. *Maladroit* is an interesting word to break apart. You know that *adroit* means *skilled* from the synonyms for *dexterous* in Group 19, and since *mal-* means *not, maladroit* means *not skilled—clumsy. Maladroit* is, of course, also the name of Weezer's fourth album, released in 2002.

Synonyms: Select the word or phrase whose meaning is closest to the word in capital letters.

1. ANGUISH
    A. suffering
    B. matrimony
    C. elation
    D. euphoria
    E. ebullience

2. RAMIFICATION
    A. ultimatum
    B. augmentation
    C. exacerbation
    D. consequence
    E. prerequisite

3. DEPRECATING
    A. plural
    B. denigrating
    C. rueful
    D. bleak
    E. implacable

4. INEPT
    A. inexorable
    B. intransigent
    C. relentless
    D. disparaging
    E. maladroit

Analogies: Select the answer choice that best completes the meaning of the sentence.

5. Clumsy is to maladroit as
    A. anguished is to suffering
    B. deprecating is to puerile
    C. rueful is to reclusive
    D. inept is to exuding
    E. gangly is to errant

6. Ramification is to effect as
    A. plural is to singular
    B. matrimony is to event
    C. crimson is to color
    D. pejorative is to criticism
    E. epiphany is to insight

Sentence Completions: Choose the word or words that, when inserted in the sentence, *best* fits the meaning of the sentence as a whole.

7. Ruefully, Hayley reviewed the _____ ramifications of her decisions and decided that she had caused her own _____.
    A. plural . . mania
    B. gloomy . . discord
    C. bleak . . anguish
    D. succinct . . demise
    E. enigmatic . . chagrin

8. In English class, we will discuss who was more _____, Trinculo or Grumio; we will examine the ways in which each character criticized himself to others.
    A. macabre
    B. inept
    C. deprecating
    D. gangly
    E. malignant

Solutions

1. **A.** *Anguished* means *suffering. Matrimony* means *marriage,* and *elation, euphoria,* and *ebullience* mean *extreme happiness.*

2. **D.** *Ramification* means *consequence. Ultimatum* means *final demand, augmentation* means *increasing, exacerbation* means *increasing and making worse,* and *prerequisite* means *something required before.*

3. **B.** *Deprecating* and *denigrating* mean *criticizing. Plural* means *more than one, rueful* means *regretful, bleak* means *gloomy,* and *implacable* means *unsatisfiable.*

4. **E.** *Inept* and *maladroit* mean *clumsy.* Use the process of elimination. *Inexorable* means *unstoppable, intransigent* and *relentless* mean *not giving in,* and *disparaging* means *criticizing.*

5. **A.** "A clumsy person is maladroit (clumsy)."
   - (A.) An anguished (suffering) person is suffering . . . yes!
   - B . A deprecating (criticizing) person is puerile (childish) . . . no, not necessarily.
   - C . A rueful (sorrowful) person is reclusive (solitary) . . . no, not necessarily.
   - D. An inept (unskilled) person is exuding (radiating) . . . no.
   - E . A gangly (tall, thin, clumsy) person is errant (stray) . . . no.

6. **D.** "Ramification means a negative effect."
   - A . Plural (more than one) means a negative singular . . . no.
   - B . Matrimony (marriage) means a negative event . . . no, Bella may think that now, but don't you think she'll change her mind?
   - C . Crimson (purplish-red) means a negative color . . . no.
   - (D.) Pejorative (critical) means a negative criticism . . . yes!
   - E . Epiphany (insight) means a negative insight . . . no, not necessarily.

7. **C.** "Ruefully, Hayley reviewed the *????* ramifications of her decisions and decided that she had caused her own <u>ramifications</u>."
   Use the process of elimination, one blank at a time. *Bleak* means *gloomy,* and *anguish* means *suffering,* so choice C works best. You have no evidence that the ramifications were *plural* (more than one), *succinct* (brief), or *enigmatic* (mysterious).

8. **C.** "In English class, we will discuss who was more <u>critical,</u> Trinculo or Grumio; we will examine the ways in which each character criticized himself to others."
   Deprecating means *critical.*

Quiz 6

I. Let's review some of the words that you've seen in Groups 26–30. Match each of the following words to the correct definition or synonym on the right. Then check the solutions on page 172.

1.	Superficial	A.	Exhausted-looking
2.	Haggard	B.	Pretense
3.	Incorrigible	C.	Impenitent
4.	Epoch	D.	Solitary
5.	Farce	E.	Shallow
6.	Morose	F.	Exuberant
7.	Reclusive	G.	Eon
8.	Boisterous	H.	Stray
9.	Euphoric	I.	Gloomy
10.	Implacable	J.	Negative effect
11.	Gangly	K.	Maladroit
12.	Errant	L.	Pejorative
13.	Ramification	M.	Ebullient
14.	Deprecating	N.	Inexorable
15.	Inept	O.	Lanky

II. Let's review several of the word parts that you've seen in Groups 26–30. Match each of the following word parts to the correct definition or synonym on the right. Then check the solutions on page 172.

16.	Super-	A.	Out
17.	Ex-	B.	Skilled
18.	Dict-	C.	Not
19.	Im-	D.	Beyond
20.	Mal-	E.	Say
21.	Adroit	F.	Not

Group 31
Coercion and Wheedling

Find each of the following words on the *Eclipse* page number provided. Based on the way each word is used in the book, guess at its definition.

1. **Hefty** (p. 445) might mean _____

_____

2. **Duress** (p. 451) might mean _____

_____

3. **Coercion** (p. 451) might mean_____

_____

4. **Wheedling** (p. 452) might mean _____

_____

5. **Dissension** (p. 453) might mean_____

_____

6. **Ulterior** (p. 455) might mean_____

_____

7. **Sidelong** (p. 456) might mean _____

_____

8. **Condescendingly** (p. 456) might mean _____

_____

Let's see how you did. Check your answers, write the exact definitions, and reread the sentence in *Eclipse* where each word appears. Then complete the drills on the next page.

1. **Hefty** (p. 445) means *large*. It also means *heavy* and *powerful;* that's why a trash bag company named their bags "Hefty," to imply that they are powerful—able to carry large, heavy loads without tearing. This also makes me think of Hefty Smurf. He's the one who loves weightlifting—he reminds me of Emmett actually! If Emmett is Hefty Smurf, then I suppose Carlisle is Papa Smurf, and Bella is Smurfette!

2. **Duress** (p. 451) means *actions that forcibly persuade someone to do something.*

3. **Coercion** (p. 451) means *actions that persuade someone to do something* and is a synonym for *duress.*

4. **Wheedling** (p. 452) means *using sweetness to persuade.* First Edward was coercing Bella to marry him, and now Bella is trying to wheedle Edward to . . . well, this is a G-rated book, so I can't tell you what she's trying to convince him to do . . . .

5. **Dissension** (p. 453) means *disagreement.*

6. **Ulterior** (p. 455) means *hidden* or *happening in the future.*

7. **Sidelong** (p. 456) means *sideways* and implies a *secret, disguised look out of the corner of one's eyes.* Synonyms: covert, furtive, indirect, oblique, sly, surreptitious. Interestingly, the opposite of *covert* (secret) is *overt* (obvious).

8. **Condescendingly** (p. 456) means *with a superior attitude.* That reminds me of the word *supercilious* (acting superior, arrogant) from Group 26. Other synonyms of *condescending* are *haughty* and *patronizing.*

Synonyms: Select the word or phrase whose meaning is closest to the word in capital letters.

Drills

1. DURESS
   - A. coercion
   - B. wheedling
   - C. anguish
   - D. ramifications
   - E. matrimony

2. WHEEDLE
   - A. patronize
   - B. disparage
   - C. persuade
   - D. denigrate
   - E. deprecate

3. DISSENSION
   - A. disagreement
   - B. anarchy
   - C. bedlam
   - D. mayhem
   - E. rumpus

4. CONDESCENDING
   - A. sidelong
   - B. furtive
   - C. oblique
   - D. surreptitious
   - E. supercilious

Analogies: Select the answer choice that best completes the meaning of the sentence.

5. Emmett is to hefty as
   - A. Bella is to patronizing
   - B. Edward is to maladroit
   - C. Jasper is to omniscient
   - D. Alice is to prophetic
   - E. Carlisle is to obtuse

6. Sidelong is to glance as
   - A. ulterior is to motive
   - B. condescending is to attitude
   - C. ramification is to effect
   - D. subterfuge is to greeting
   - E. reproach is to scolding

Sentence Completions: Choose the word that, when inserted in the sentence, *best* fits the meaning of the sentence as a whole.

7. Luis saw the ulterior motives of the salesman and would not succumb to any types of coercion or _____, no matter how subtle.
   - A. dissension
   - B. correspondence
   - C. entente
   - D. accord
   - E. wheedling

8. Harry risked a(n) _____ glance at Ginny, knowing that if Ron caught him, there'd be trouble.
   - A. hefty
   - B. surreptitious
   - C. wheedling
   - D. arduous
   - E. plaintive

1. **A.** *Duress* and *coercion* mean *using force to persuade,* so choice A is best. *Wheedling* is close, but means *using flattery to persuade, anguish* means *suffering, ramifications* means *consequences,* and *matrimony* means *marriage.*

2. **C.** *Wheedle* means *persuade. Patronize, disparage, denigrate,* and *deprecate* mean *treat with inferiority.*

3. **A.** *Dissension* means *disagreement. Anarchy, bedlam, mayhem,* and *rumpus* mean *disorder.*

4. **E.** *Condescending* and *supercilious* mean *looking down on others. Sidelong, furtive, oblique,* and *surreptitious* mean *secretive.*

5. **D.** "Emmett is hefty (large and powerful)."
   A. Bella is patronizing (condescending) . . . no, not all the time.
   B. Edward is maladroit (clumsy) . . . ahem.
   C. Jasper is omniscient (all-knowing) . . . no.
   D. Alice is prophetic (predicting the future) . . . yes!
   E. Carlisle is obtuse (thick, slow to understand) . . . no way!

6. **A.** "Sidelong is a secret glance."
   A. Ulterior is a secret motive . . . yes.
   B. Condescending is a secret attitude . . . no, it's a *critical attitude.*
   C. Ramification is a secret effect . . . no, it's a *negative effect.*
   D. Subterfuge (trickery) is a secret greeting . . . no.
   E. Reproach (scolding) is a secret scolding . . . no.
   Notice that if you used the sentence "sidelong is a type of look," then several answer choices work. When that happens make your sentence more specific. See if you can define the first word using the second, "sidelong is a **secret** look." Remember to try all the choices; don't just choose the first one that seems to work.

7. **E.** "Luis saw the ulterior motives of the salesman and would not succumb to any types of coercion or <u>coercion</u>, no matter how subtle."
   Wheedling means *flattering to persuade* and fits best. It is like coercion, but subtler, so it fits the evidence in the sentence perfectly.

8. **B.** "Harry risked a(n) <u>????</u> glance at Ginny, knowing that if Ron caught him, there'd be trouble."
   If you can't think of a word to fill the blank, use the process of elimination. *Surreptitious* means *secret.* You have no evidence that it was a *hefty* (large), *wheedling* (persuading), *arduous* (difficult), or *plaintive* (sad) glance, only that it was secret—he didn't want Ron to see.

Exultant Edward

Find each of the following words on the *Eclipse* page number provided. Based on the way each word is used in the book, guess at its definition.

1. **Fretting** (p. 456) might mean _____

   _____

2. **Complacently** (p. 456) might mean _____

   _____

3. **Brusquely** (p. 457) might mean _____

   _____

4. **Feigning** (p. 458) might mean _____

   _____

5. **Exultant** (p. 459) might mean _____

   _____

6. **Gooey** (p. 460) might mean _____

   _____

7. **Enormity** (p. 462) might mean _____

   _____

8. **Unscrupulous** (p. 469) might mean _____

   _____

Let's see how you did. Check your answers, write the exact definitions, and reread the sentence in *Eclipse* where each word appears. Then complete the drills on the next page.

1. **Fretting** (p. 456) means *worrying.*

2. **Complacently** (p. 456) means *in a self-satisfied way.* For an extra example of this word, let's reference the wisdom of *One Tree Hill* sage Nathan Scott, " . . . we just don't recognize the significant moments of our lives while they're happening. We grow complacent with ideas, or things or people and we take them for granted and it's usually not until that thing is about to be taken away from you that you've realized . . . how much you need it, how much you love it." (The WB, "Everyday Is a Sunday Evening," 2003)

3. **Brusquely** (p. 457) means *abruptly or rudely.* Edward is hurt by Bella's attitude toward marriage and the ring, so he's a bit snippy. Synonyms: curtly, gruffly, offhandedly, tersely.

4. **Feigning** (p. 458) means *pretending.* Bella is trying to **pretend** she was not stunned by how beautiful the ring is. *Feigning* looks and sounds a lot like the word *feinting* which means *faking a movement,* like when a lacrosse player *feints* (fakes) left to throw off a defender and break free for a shot on goal. *Feigning* is also similar in meaning to *subterfuge* (trickery) from Group 1 and *farce* from Group 27.

5. **Exultant** (p. 459) means *thrilled* and was a synonym for *exuberant, ecstatic,* and *euphoric* in Groups 13, 24, and 28. The other synonyms were *buoyant, ebullient, elated, jubilant,* and *rapturous.*

6. **Gooey** (p. 460) means *sticky* or, in this case, *emotionally sappy.* You probably know this already, but I included it here for two reasons. First, I love this scene. It always makes me cry. And second, standardized tests love to test the synonyms for *gooey:* cloying, mawkish, saccharine, sentimental, treacly. I saw the word *treacly* stump nearly everyone on a recent SAT—everyone except people who recognized the connection to Harry Potter's favorite **sweet and sappy** desert, **treacle** tart!

7. **Enormity** (p. 462) means *hugeness or importance—enormousness.*

8. **Unscrupulous** (p. 469) means *stopping at nothing, immoral,* or *unfair.* Synonyms: conscienceless, reprobate, shameless, unethical.

Synonyms: Select the word or phrase whose meaning is closest to the word in capital letters.

1. COMPLACENT
   A. fretting
   B. curt
   C. gruff
   D. offhanded
   E. self-satisfied

2. BRUSQUE
   A. exuberant
   B. ecstatic
   C. terse
   D. euphoric
   E. buoyant

3. EXULTANT
   A. ebullient
   B. cloying
   C. mawkish
   D. saccharine
   E. unscrupulous

4. GOOEY
   A. reprobate
   B. treacly
   C. hefty
   D. obtuse
   E. surreptitious

Analogies: Select the answer choice that best completes the meaning of the sentence.

5. Pacify is to fretting as
   A. coerce is to unscrupulous
   B. wheedle is to reprobate
   C. reproach is to exultant
   D. beseech is to supercilious
   E. cheer up is to morose

6. Villain is to unscrupulous as
   A. ramification is to saccharine
   B. vampire is to generic
   C. werewolf is to haggard
   D. valedictorian is to obtuse
   E. recluse is to solitary

Sentence Completions: Choose the word or words that, when inserted in the sentence, *best* fits the meaning of the sentence as a whole.

7. Many critics feel that Cavallo's films are not so sentimental as to be called _____.
   A. brusque
   B. terse
   C. treacly
   D. conscienceless
   E. maladroit

8. The judge believed that the _____ of the crime demonstrated the thief's _____ nature.
   A. enormity .. unscrupulous
   B. complacency .. deprecating
   C. feigning .. pejorative
   D. ramifications .. bleak
   E. ineptness .. patronizing

1. **E.** *Complacent* means *self-satisfied. Fretting* means *worrying;* and *curt,*
   gruff, and *offhanded* mean *abrupt or rude.*
2. **C.** *Brusque* and *terse* mean *abrupt or rude. Exuberant, ecstatic, euphoric,*
   and *buoyant* mean *very excited.*
3. **A.** *Exultant* and *ebullient* mean *very excited. Cloying, mawkish,* and
   saccharine mean *overly sentimental. Unscrupulous* means *stopping at*
   nothing, immoral, or *unfair.*
4. **B.** *Gooey* and *treacly* mean *overly sentimental. Reprobate* means *immoral,*
   hefty means *large, obtuse* means *thick and slow to understand,* and
   surreptitious means *secret.*
5. **E.** "You might try to pacify (soothe) a fretting (worrying) person."
   - A. You might try to coerce (pressure) an unscrupulous
     (immoral) person . . . no.
   - B. You might try to wheedle (pressure) a reprobate (immoral)
     person . . . no.
   - C. You might try to reproach (scold) an exultant (thrilled)
     person . . . no.
   - D. You might try to beseech (beg) a supercilious (arrogant)
     person . . . no.
   - (E.) You might try to cheer up a morose (gloomy) person . . . yes.
     The words in the correct answer should be clearly and directly
   related.
6. **E.** "A villain is usually unscrupulous (immoral)."
   - A. A ramification (consequence) is usually saccharine (too
     sentimental) . . . no.
   - B. A vampire is usually generic (general) . . . no, they're all
     pretty different.
   - C. A werewolf is usually haggard (unhealthy looking) . . . no,
     unless maybe s/he's been up all night looking for vampires.
   - D. A valedictorian (highest-ranked student) is usually obtuse
     (slow to understand) . . . no.
   - (E.) A recluse (solitary person) is usually solitary . . . yes.
7. **C.** "Many critics feel that Cavallo's films are not so sentimental
   as to be called _so sentimental_."
   Treacly means *too sentimental.*
8. **A.** "The judge believed that the _____ of the crime
   demonstrated the thief's _____ nature."
   About once per test, the SAT gives you a sentence completion
   in which there is no evidence for the words you need for the blanks.
   In this case, decide if the words should have similar or opposite
   meanings. In this question, "the _____ of the crime demonstrated
   the thief's _____," so the words must be related. Use the process of
   elimination looking for the pair of similar words that fit best into the
   sentence. The words in choice A fit perfectly into the blanks.

Group 33

Glacial Wind

Find each of the following words on the *Eclipse* page number provided. Based on the way each word is used in the book, guess at its definition.

1. **Clerical** (p. 469) might mean _____

   _____

2. **Pleasantry** (p. 473) might mean _____

   _____

3. **Alpha** (p. 482) might mean _____

   _____

4. **Beta** (p. 482) might mean _____

   _____

5. **Evasively** (p. 483) might mean _____

   _____

6. **Lineage** (p. 483) might mean _____

   _____

7. **Glacier** (p. 485) might mean _____

   _____

8. **Lee** (p. 485) might mean _____

   _____

Let's see how you did. Check your answers, write the exact definitions,
and reread the sentence in *Eclipse* where each word appears. Then
complete the drills on the next page.

1. **Clerical** (p. 469) means *pertaining to a religious minister.* Synonym:
   sacerdotal. *Sacerdotal* is a super high-level word that is easy to
   remember since it looks a lot like *sacred,* meaning *related to religion.*
   In fact, *sacr-* implies *holy.* Oddly enough, the word *clerical* also means
   relating to office work, as in the **clerical** staff who make photocopies
   and type memos in *Mad Men* or *The Office.*

2. **Pleasantry** (p. 473) means *pleasant, unimportant conversation.*

3. **Alpha** (p. 482) refers to the *first letter of the Greek alphabet* and
   therefore refers to *the one in the first position—the one in charge.*

4. **Beta** (p. 482) refers to the *second letter of the Greek alphabet* and
   therefore to *the one in the second position.* Bella invented using *beta*
   to mean the *second in command,* but she is not the first to make up
   a term. Shakespeare invented the words *multitudinous* (*many,* like
   multifarious from Group 23) and *sanctimonious* (*acting superior* from
   Group 13), Dr. Seuss invented the word *nerd,* Homer Simpson
   invented the word *D'oh!,* which is now actually listed in the
   Oxford English Dictionary, and, of course, Bart Simpson invented
   the word *craptastic,* which is not yet in the dictionary.

5. **Evasively** (p. 483) means *avoidingly.*

6. **Lineage** (p. 483) means *ancestors.* Jacob describes the word, "Why
   should it matter who your grandpa was, right?" Standardized tests
   always do that, too; they describe difficult words nearby in the
   passage.

7. **Glacier** (p. 485) means *a massive, slow-moving river of ice,* and comes
   from the French word, *glace,* for ice. That helps you remember the
   SAT word *glacial,* which means *cold* or *unfriendly.*

8. **Lee** (p. 485) means *sheltered from weather.* It was still mighty windy
   there, but Edward chose the side of the peak that was more
   sheltered from the glacial wind.

Synonyms: Select the word or phrase whose meaning is closest to the word in capital letters.

Drills

1. CLERICAL
   A. pleasant
   B. sacerdotal
   C. evasive
   D. multitudinous
   E. sanctimonious

2. EVASIVE
   A. alpha
   B. beta
   C. multifarious
   D. complacent
   E. avoiding

3. LINEAGE
   A. glacier
   B. enormity
   C. epoch
   D. ancestors
   E. anguish

4. GLACIAL
   A. clerical
   B. not euphoric
   C. not gregarious
   D. not impromptu
   E. adroit

Analogies: Select the answer choice that best completes the meaning of the sentence.

5. Furtive is to evade as
   A. sacerdotal is to exude
   B. feigning is to trick
   C. feinting is to denigrate
   D. glacial is to admonish
   E. sanctimonious is to coerce

6. Multitudinous is to abundant as
   A. arduous is to cloying
   B. brusque is to Herculean
   C. terse is to mawkish
   D. treacly is to saccharine
   E. unscrupulous is to sidelong

Sentence Completions: Choose the word that, when inserted in the sentence, *best* fits the meaning of the sentence as a whole.

7. Ali was generally gregarious and comfortable with both _____ and deep conversations at parties.
   A. lineage
   B. pleasantries
   C. fretting
   D. enormity
   E. dissension

8. To avoid the glacial wind, Alleb hiked to the _____ side of the hill.
   A. evasive
   B. alpha
   C. beta
   D. sacerdotal
   E. lee

1. **B.** *Clerical* and *sacerdotal* mean *relating to a religious minister. Evasive* means *avoiding, multitudinous* means *many,* and *sanctimonious* means *acting superior.*

2. **E.** *Evasive* means *avoiding. Alpha* means *first, beta* means *second, multifarious* means *many and varied,* and *complacent* means *self-satisfied.*

3. **D.** *Lineage* means *ancestors. Glacier* means *river of ice, enormity* means *hugeness, epoch* means *long period of history,* and *anguish* means *suffering. Epoch* has to do with history, but *ancestors* is a much more direct synonym to *lineage.*

4. **C.** *Glacial* means *cold or unfriendly,* so *not gregarious* (unfriendly, not social) is the best answer. *Clerical* means *related to a religious minister, euphoric* means *thrilled, impromptu* means *spontaneous,* and *adroit* means *skilled.*

5. **B.** "A furtive (secret) action might be used to evade (avoid) something."

   A. A sacerdotal (religious) action might be used to exude (radiate) something . . . no.

   B. A feigning (faking) action might be used to trick something . . . yes.

   C. A feinting (faking) action might be used to denigrate (criticize) something . . . no.

   D. A glacial (very cold, unfriendly) action might be used to admonish (scold) something . . . maybe, but choice B is a more clear and direct relationship.

   E. A sanctimonious (arrogant) action might be used to coerce (persuade) something . . . maybe, but again, choice B is a more clear and direct relationship.

6. **D.** "Multitudinous (many) means abundant (many)."

   A. Arduous (difficult) means cloying (too sentimental) . . . no.

   B. Brusque (abrupt) means Herculean (requiring strength) . . . no.

   C. Terse (abrupt) means mawkish (too sentimental) . . . no.

   D. Treacly (too sentimental) means saccharine (too sentimental) . . . yes!

   E. Unscrupulous (immoral) means sidelong (secret) . . . no.
      Don't convince yourself that a choice that does not make sense to you is correct; choose an answer that has a clear relationship.

7. **B.** "Ali was generally gregarious and comfortable with both *gregariousness* and deep conversations at parties."
      Use the process of elimination. *Pleasantries* means *unimportant conversation* and works best.

8. **E.** "To avoid the glacial wind, Alleb hiked to the *????* side of the hill."
      Lee means *sheltered from weather.*

Group 34
Civilized Wrangling

Find each of the following words on the *Eclipse* page number provided. Based on the way each word is used in the book, guess at its definition.

1. **Acute** (p. 485) might mean _____

_____

2. **Convulsion** (p. 489) might mean _____

_____

3. **Mongrel** (p. 492) might mean _____

_____

4. **Wrangled** (p. 492) might mean _____

_____

5. **Vindictive** (p. 492) might mean _____

_____

6. **Musky** (p. 492) might mean _____

_____

7. **Defiant** (p. 494) might mean _____

_____

8. **Civilized** (p. 497) might mean _____

_____

Let's see how you did. Check your answers, write the exact definitions,
and reread the sentence in *Eclipse* where each word appears. Then
complete the drills on the next page.

1. **Acute** (p. 485) in this case means *severe*. It can also mean *sharp*.
   And as Mr. Varner, Bella's trigonometry teacher, can tell you, it
   also refers to *an angle that is less than 90 degrees.*

2. **Convulsion** (p. 489) means *spasm.*

3. **Mongrel** (p. 492) means *mix of breeds.* Synonym: mutt. *Mongrel*
   can be used as a technical term or as an insult. Guess which way
   Edward meant it?!

4. **Wrangled** (p. 492) means *argued, usually about something complex.*
   The problems between Edward and Jacob are definitely pretty
   complex. *Wrangle* also means *round up,* as in **wrangle** a herd of
   cattle. That's why a cowboy is sometimes called a *wrangler.*

5. **Vindictive** (p. 492) means *revengeful.* Bella is getting **revenge** for
   Jacob's crack about warming up her lips. Synonym: vengeful.

6. **Musky** (p. 492) refers to *an outdoorsy, masculine scent. Musk* is
   actually an *ingredient in colognes that comes from a secretion of the male
   musk deer.*

7. **Defiant** (p. 494) means *defying, resisting,* or *challenging.* That's
   why *Defiant* was the title for punk band Vice Squad's 2006 album
   and the name of a starship in the *Star Trek* saga. Synonyms:
   dissenting, insubordinate, intransigent, noncompliant, obstinate,
   obstreperous, recalcitrant, subversive, truculent (very defiant).
   Those are some very fine standardized test words!

8. **Civilized** (p. 497) means *well-mannered.* It can also mean *socially
   or culturally advanced.* Synonyms: polished, urbane. Here's another
   question from your fantasy English class: Who would you say is
   more civilized, polished, and urbane, Carlisle or Aro? Discuss with
   your friends. I'd say the answer is obvious, but not everyone agrees
   with me.

Synonyms: Select the word or phrase whose meaning is closest to the word in capital letters.

1. ACUTE
   A. musky
   B. severe
   C. dissenting
   D. insubordinate
   E. intransigent

2. WRANGLE
   A. convulse
   B. fret
   C. argue
   D. feign
   E. condescend

3. VINDICTIVE
   A. vengeful
   B. sharp
   C. noncompliant
   D. obstinate
   E. obstreperous

4. DEFIANT
   A. civilized
   B. polished
   C. urbane
   D. recalcitrant
   E. sacerdotal

Analogies: Select the answer choice that best completes the meaning of the sentence.

5. Truculent is to recalcitrant as
   A. dissenting is to urbane
   B. obstinate is to intransigent
   C. obstreperous is to polished
   D. subversive is to vindictive
   E. musky is to saccharine

6. Brusque is to urbane as
   A. subterfuge is to artifice
   B. stringent is to stern
   C. conditional is to qualified
   D. judicious is to sagacious
   E. truculent is to acquiescent

Sentence Completions: Choose the word or words that, when inserted in the sentence, *best* fits the meaning of the sentence as a whole.

7. Ms. Darbus suffered several _____ when she discovered students texting during her class, and she promised _____ for their insubordination.
   A. wranglings . . vigilance
   B. epidemics . . jibes
   C. convulsions . . vengeance
   D. consternations . . adulation
   E. exultations . . abstraction

8. Nadine said that the song she wrote was like _____; it had influences from classical, hip hop, country, and jazz.
   A. an antiquity
   B. a rebuttal
   C. an armistice
   D. a satellite
   E. a mongrel

1. **B.** *Acute* means *severe*. *Musky* refers to a *woodsy scent*. *Dissenting,*
   insubordinate, and *intransigent* mean *defying*.
2. **C.** *Wrangle* means *argue*. *Convulse* means *spasm, fret* means *worry,*
   feign means *fake,* and *condescend* means *look down on*.
3. **A.** *Vindictive* and *vengeful* mean *revengeful*. *Noncompliant, obstinate,*
   and *obstreperous* mean *defying*.
4. **D.** *Defiant* and *recalcitrant* mean *defying*. *Polished* and *urbane* mean
   civilized, and *sacerdotal* means *relating to religion*.
5. **B.** "Truculent (very defiant) is similar to recalcitrant (defiant)."
   A. Dissenting (defiant) is similar to urbane (well-mannered) . . .
      no.
   B. Obstinate (stubborn) is similar to intransigent (stubborn) . . .
      yes!
   C. Obstreperous (defiant) is similar to polished . . . no.
   D. Subversive (defiant) is similar to vindictive (revengeful) . . . no.
   E. Musky (woodsy scented) is similar to saccharine (too
      sentimental) . . . no.
6. **E.** "Brusque (rude, abrupt) is the opposite of urbane
   (well-mannered)."
      Look at all these awesome words that you've learned!
   A. Subterfuge (trickery) is the opposite of artifice (trickery) . . . no.
   B. Stringent (strict) is the opposite of stern (strict) . . . no.
   C. Conditional (with conditions) is the opposite of qualified
      (with conditions) . . . no.
   D. Judicious (wise) is the opposite of sagacious (wise) . . . no.
   E. Truculent (very defiant) is the opposite of acquiescent
      (willing) . . . yes.
7. **C.** "Ms. Darbus suffered several *sufferings* when she discovered
   students texting during her class, and she promised *punishment*
   for their insubordination."
      Use the process of elimination, one blank at a time.
   Convulsions means *spasms,* and *vengeance* means *revenge*.
8. **E.** "Nadine said that the song she wrote was like *it had many*
   influences; it had influences from classical, hip hop, country,
   and jazz."
      Mongrel means *mix of breeds* and sounds a bit weird in the
   sentence, but it's the best of the choices. Make sure to answer
   the question based on evidence in the sentence. The song may
   have been *an antiquity* (old thing), *a rebuttal* (denial), or *an armistice*
   (truce), but you have evidence **only** that it had many "influences."

Solutions

Newborn Horde

Find each of the following words on the *Eclipse* page number provided. Based on the way each word is used in the book, guess at its definition.

1. **Conspires** (p. 502) might mean _____

_____

2. **Inert** (p. 507) might mean _____

_____

3. **Impassively** (p. 508) might mean _____

_____

4. **Perverse** (p. 509) might mean _____

_____

5. **Horde** (p. 509) might mean _____

_____

6. **Differentiate** (p. 512) might mean _____

_____

7. **Mollified** (p. 512) might mean _____

_____

8. **Reservations** (p. 513) might mean _____

_____

Let's see how you did. Check your answers, write the exact definitions, and reread the sentence in *Eclipse* where each word appears. Then complete the drills on the next page.

1. **Conspires** (p. 502) means *plots.* This is a great word to break apart. *Con-* means *with* or *together,* as in *conjoined* (joined together), and *spir-* refers to *breathe,* so *conspire* means *breathe together,* like two people huddled close together whispering and **plotting.** *Con-* also helps you with great words like *convivial* (*viv-* refers to *life,* so **with** *life—lively*) and *connubial* (*nub-* refers to *matrimony* (marriage), so **with** *marriage—related to marriage*). BTW, I love the next page in *Eclipse* where Edward admits that he could like Jacob.

2. **Inert** (p. 507) means *inactive.* Bella means that, even asleep and **inactive,** Jacob is mighty strong.

3. **Impassively** (p. 508) means *without emotion.* Synonyms: apathetically, dispassionately, indifferently.

4. **Perverse** (p. 509) means *deviant,* like in *Gossip Girl* when Blair arranges for Serena, Nate, and Chuck to get together, to which Chuck says, "Maybe this is Blair's idea of a **perverse** double-date." (The CW, "Woman on the Verge," 2008)

5. **Horde** (p. 509) means *mob.*

6. **Differentiate** (p. 512) means *tell the difference between.* Synonyms: discriminate, distinguish.

7. **Mollified** (p. 512) means *soothed* and was a synonym for *appease, placate,* and *alleviate,* in Groups 5, 8, and 10. The other synonyms were *abate, allay, ameliorate, assuage, conciliate, mitigate, pacify, propitiate,* and *temper.*

8. **Reservations** (p. 513) in this case means *conditions* or *qualifications.*

Drills

1. CONSPIRE
   A. differentiate
   B. discriminate
   C. distinguish
   D. qualify
   E. plot

3. IMPASSIVE
   A. abated
   B. ameliorated
   C. assuaged
   D. indifferent
   E. propitiated

2. INERT
   A. convivial
   B. inactive
   C. impassive
   D. apathetic
   E. dispassionate

4. MOLLIFY
   A. convulse
   B. wrangle
   C. conciliate
   D. acquiesce
   E. wane

Analogies: Select the answer choice that best completes the meaning of the sentence.

5. Impassive is to ardent as
   A. dispassionate is to perverse
   B. abashed is to allayed
   C. narcissistic is to keen
   D. marred is to conditional
   E. apathetic is to zealous

6. Horde is to profusion as
   A. neophyte is to reservation
   B. mongrel is to mix
   C. glacier is to hyperbole
   D. lineage is to surfeit
   E. ramification is to loathing

Sentence Completions: Choose the word or words that, when inserted in the sentence, *best* fits the meaning of the sentence as a whole.

7. Though he tried to appear _____, Wallace was terrified by the enemy _____ that faced his army in battle.
   A. reserved .. hemorrhage
   B. reclusive .. predators
   C. obtuse .. entente
   D. impassive .. horde
   E. macabre .. vendetta

8. Billy's advisor recommended him to Harvard University without _____; she believed that he was the perfect Harvard applicant.
   A. qualification
   B. perversion
   C. discrimination
   D. conspiring
   E. propinquity

1. **E.** *Conspire* means *plot. Differentiate, discriminate,* and *distinguish* mean *tell the difference between,* and *qualify* means *restrict.*

2. **B.** *Inert* means *inactive. Convivial* means *lively. Impassive, apathetic,* and *dispassionate* mean *without emotion.*

3. **D.** *Impassive* and *indifferent* mean *not emotional. Abated, ameliorated, assuaged,* and *propitiated* mean *soothed or lessened.*

4. **C.** *Mollify* and *conciliate* mean *soothe. Convulse* means *spasm, wrangle* means *argue, acquiesce* means *give in,* and *wane* means *decrease. Acquiesce* is the second best answer; *acquiescing* (giving in) might *mollify* (soothe) someone whom you're debating, but *conciliate* (soothe) is a much closer synonym.

5. **E.** "Impassive (lacking emotion) is the opposite of ardent (passionate)."
   A. Dispassionate (lacking emotion) is the opposite of perverse (deviant) . . . no.
   B. Abashed (embarrassed) is the opposite of allayed (soothed) . . . no.
   C. Narcissistic (vain) is the opposite of keen (passionate) . . . no.
   D. Marred (spoiled) is the opposite of conditional (restricted) . . . no.
   E. Apathetic (lacking emotion) is the opposite of zealous (passionate) . . . yes!

6. **B.** "A horde (mob) is a profusion (abundance) of something."
   A. A neophyte (newbie) is a reservation (condition) of something . . . no.
   B. A mongrel (mutt) is a mix of something . . . yes, a mutt is a blend.
   C. A glacier (river of ice) is a hyperbole (exaggeration) of something . . . no.
   D. A lineage (ancestors) is a surfeit (abundance) of something . . . no.
   E. A ramification (consequence) is a loathing (hatred) of something . . . no.

7. **D.** "Though he tried to appear <u>not terrified</u>, Wallace was terrified by the enemy <u>????</u> that faced his army in battle."
   Impassive means *unemotional,* and *horde* means *mob,* so choice D is best.

8. **A.** "Billy's advisor recommended him to Harvard University without <u>concern</u>; she believed that he was the perfect Harvard applicant."
   Qualification means *condition* and fits best.

Quiz 7

I. Let's review some of the words that you've seen in Groups 31–35. Match each of the following words to the correct definition or synonym on the right. Then check the solutions on page 172.

1. Duress	A. Supercilious
2. Dissension	B. Saccharine
3. Condescending	C. Coercion
4. Brusque	D. Multifarious
5. Exultant	E. Severe
6. Gooey	F. Terse
7. Clerical	G. Disagreement
8. Multitudinous	H. Ebullient
9. Glacial	I. Unfriendly
10. Acute	J. Apathetic
11. Defiant	K. Sacerdotal
12. Civilized	L. Inactive
13. Inert	M. Assuage
14. Impassive	N. Urbane
15. Mollify	O. Truculent

II. Let's review several of the word parts that you've seen in Groups 31–35. Match each of the following word parts to the correct definition or synonym on the right. Then check the solutions on page 172.

16. Glace	A. Life
17. Sacr-	B. With
18. Con-	C. Marital
19. Spir-	D. Ice
20. Viv-	E. Breathe
21. Nub-	F. Holy

Group 36

Fissure

Find each of the following words on the *Eclipse* page number provided. Based on the way each word is used in the book, guess at its definition.

1. **Medusa** (p. 518) might mean _____

   _____

2. **Hackles** (p. 520) might mean _____

   _____

3. **Tangible** (p. 529) might mean _____

   _____

4. **Fissure** (p. 529) might mean _____

   _____

5. **Avalanche** (p. 531) might mean _____

   _____

6. **Stridently** (p. 536) might mean _____

   _____

7. **Soprano** (p. 544) might mean _____

   _____

8. **Ferocious** (p. 545) might mean _____

   _____

Let's see how you did. Check your answers, write the exact definitions, and reread the sentence in *Eclipse* where each word appears. Then complete the drills on the next page.

1. **Medusa** (p. 518) refers to the *Greek mythological female monster who had snakes for hair.* Anyone who looked at Medusa's face would turn to stone. Bella tends to be a bit *deprecating* (critical); I doubt her hair looked that bad.

2. **Hackles** (p. 520) are *the hairs on the back of a dog (or wolf) or person's head that straighten when the animal or person is angry or frightened.* Those hairs really do stand up when people are alarmed, which is pretty interesting.

3. **Tangible** (p. 529) means *touchable or real.* Synonyms: corporeal, palpable, tactile. *Tangible* relates to the sense of touch. Standardized tests love to test the fancy names for the senses: touch = tactition, taste = gustation, hearing = audition, smell = olfaction.

4. **Fissure** (p. 529) means *crack.* This is another Team Edward/Team Jacob moment. The fissure line divides the part of Bella that is in love with Edward from the part that is in love with Jacob. You know who has the smaller portion . . . though I think the smaller part is really Renesme waiting to be born. That would explain the love that Bella feels for Jacob even though she wants to be with Edward. Synonyms: breach, chasm, cleft, crevasse, crevice, fault, fracture, rift, rupture.

5. **Avalanche** (p. 531) means *massive sliding of ice, rock, or snow.* This reminds me of the words *cascade, cataract, deluge, inundation, spate, and torrent,* which mean *outpouring* or *flood,* from Group 14.

6. **Stridently** (p. 536) means *loudly and harshly.* Great SAT, ACT, GED, and SSAT synonyms for *strident*: clamorous, grating, obstreperous, rasping, raucous, shrill, vociferous.

7. **Soprano** (p. 544) means the *highest singing voice.* Remember tenor (the highest **male** singing voice) from Group 20?

8. **Ferocious** (p. 545) sounds like *fury* and means *fierce and violent.* Synonyms: merciless, ruthless, savage.

Synonyms: Select the word or phrase whose meaning is closest to the word in capital letters.

1. TANGIBLE
   A. tactile
   B. clamorous
   C. grating
   D. obstreperous
   E. vociferous

2. FISSURE
   A. Medusa
   B. hackles
   C. chasm
   D. torrent
   E. cascade

3. AVALANCHE
   A. deluge
   B. soprano
   C. tenor
   D. fury
   E. crevice

4. STRIDENT
   A. ferocious
   B. merciless
   C. inert
   D. apathetic
   E. shrill

Analogies: Select the answer choice that best completes the meaning of the sentence.

5. Avalanche is to ice as
   A. cleft is to mountain
   B. inundation is to water
   C. lee is to wind
   D. cascade is to hackles
   E. cataract is to Medusa

6. Tangible is to felt as
   A. tactile is to heard
   B. palpable is to smelled
   C. audible is to heard
   D. olfactory is to seen
   E. strident is to ferocious

Sentence Completions: Choose the word that, when inserted in the sentence, *best* fits the meaning of the sentence as a whole.

7. As Percy approached the Medusa, she let out a(n) _____ yell, and the hackles on Percy's neck rose.
   A. ruptured
   B. tangible
   C. grating
   D. impassive
   E. mollified

8. The group's fear of falling was almost _____ as they approached the large fissure in the rock face that they climbed.
   A. savage
   B. breached
   C. convivial
   D. assuaged
   E. palpable

Solutions

1. **A.** *Tangible* and *tactile* mean *touchable*. *Clamorous, grating, obstreperous,* and *vociferous* mean *loud and harsh*.

2. **C.** *Fissure* and *chasm* mean *crack*. *Medusa* is *a mythological woman with snakes for hair, hackles* are *neck hairs,* and *torrent* and *cascade* mean *waterfall*.

3. **A.** *Avalanche* and *deluge* mean *huge flow of water or ice*. *Soprano* is *the highest singing voice, tenor* is the *highest male voice, fury* means *anger,* and *crevice* means *crack*.

4. **E.** Use the process of elimination. *Strident* and *shrill* mean *loud and harsh*. *Ferocious* and *merciless* mean *fierce, inert* means *inactive,* and *apathetic* means *lacking emotion*.

5. **B.** "An avalanche is a huge slide of ice."
   A. A cleft (crack) is a huge slide of mountain . . . no.
   (B.) An inundation (flood) is a huge slide of water . . . maybe.
   C. A lee (sheltered) is a huge slide of wind . . . no.
   D. A cascade (waterfall) is a huge slide of hackles (neck hairs) . . . no!
   E. A cataract (waterfall) is a huge slide of Medusa (monster) . . . no.
   This type of relationship, "_____ is a huge _____" shows up quite a bit on the SSAT. Choice B is best.

6. **C.** "Something tangible (touchable) can be felt."
   A. Something tactile (touchable) can be heard . . . not necessarily.
   B. Something palpable (touchable) can be smelled . . . not necessarily.
   (C.) Something audible (hearable) can be heard . . . yes!
   D. Something olfactory (smellable) can be seen . . . not necessarily.
   E. Something strident (loud and harsh) can be ferocious . . . maybe.
   Choice C is best; it has the most direct and clear relationship.

7. **C.** "As Percy approached the Medusa, she let out a(n) _scary_ yell, and the hackles on Percy's neck rose."
   Grating means *loud and harsh* and fits best.

8. **E.** "The group's fear of falling was almost _????_ as they approached the large fissure in the rock face that they climbed."
   Palpable means *touchable* or *real,* and is the best answer. Let's review the other choices. *Savage* means *fierce, breached* means *cracked, convivial* means *friendly,* and *assuaged* means *soothed*.

Group 37

Pyre

Find each of the following words on the *Eclipse* page number provided.
Based on the way each word is used in the book, guess at its definition.

1. **Sashayed** (p. 545) might mean _____

   _____

2. **Lithely** (p. 545) might mean _____

   _____

3. **Grating** (p. 546) might mean _____

   _____

4. **Pyre** (p. 555) might mean _____

   _____

5. **Aside** (p. 555) might mean _____

   _____

6. **Offhand** (p. 558) might mean _____

   _____

7. **Sentient** (p. 558) might mean _____

   _____

8. **Blasé** (p. 559) might mean _____

   _____

Let's see how you did. Check your answers, write the exact definitions, and reread the sentence in *Eclipse* where each word appears. Then complete the drills on the next page.

1. **Sashayed** (p. 545) means *strutted casually and confidently.* This word actually comes from the sashay part of square dancing when partners **circle each other taking sideways steps,** and that's pretty much what Edward and Victoria are doing, minus the square dance part. Even more appropriately, the word *sashayed* originally comes from the word *chased!*

2. **Lithely** (p. 545) means *gracefully.* Synonyms for *lithe:* agile, deft, limber, lissome, lithesome, nimble, supple, willowy. Some of these synonyms were also synonyms for *dexterous* in Group 19, which means *graceful and skilled.* The opposite of *lithe* and *dexterous* is *maladroit* (clumsy), which you learned as a synonym for *inept* (clumsy and unskilled) in Group 30.

3. **Grating** (p. 546) in this case means *loud and harsh* and is a great chance to review the terrific SAT and ACT words *clamorous, obstreperous, rasping, raucous, shrill, strident,* and *vociferous* from Group 36. Sorry to get so excited about vocabulary during such an intense and violent scene.

4. **Pyre** (p. 555) means *a heap of stuff to burn, often at a funeral.*

5. **Aside** (p. 555) means *whispered remark.*

6. **Offhand** (p. 558) means *nonchalant, often to the point of being rude.* Bella was not being rude; she was just trying to *feign* (fake) being calm—though she did snort at Edward, which can seem pretty rude. Synonyms: aloof, blasé, cavalier, dismissive, glib, indifferent, insouciant, nonchalant, perfunctory.

7. **Sentient** (p. 558) means *living and feeling,* since *sent-* means *feel* as in *sentiment* (feeling).

8. **Blasé** (p. 559) means *bored and nonchalant,* like someone shrugging their shoulders saying "been there, done that." Standardized tests love the synonyms *surfeited* and *jaded.* Remember that *surfeit* means *overabundance,* so *surfeited* is *having had an overabundance and becoming **bored** with it.*

Synonyms: Select the word or phrase whose meaning is closest to the word in capital letters.

1. LITHE
   A. clamorous
   B. obstreperous
   C. lissome
   D. raucous
   E. vociferous

2. GRATING
   A. rasping
   B. aloof
   C. insouciant
   D. cavalier
   E. perfunctory

3. OFFHAND
   A. sentient
   B. agile
   C. deft
   D. nimble
   E. dismissive

4. BLASÉ
   A. apathetic
   B. limber
   C. lissome
   D. dexterous
   E. maladroit

Analogies: Select the answer choice that best completes the meaning of the sentence.

5. Sashay is to confident as
   A. strut is to fast
   B. amble is to leisurely
   C. jog is to slow
   D. walk is to obstreperous
   E. offhand is to tense

6. Blasé is to circumspect as
   A. vociferous is to placid
   B. lithe is to dexterous
   C. haggard is to belligerent
   D. torrent is to inundation
   E. incredulous is to dubious

Sentence Completions: Choose the word or words that, when inserted in the sentence, *best* fits the meaning of the sentence as a whole.

7. Alice lithely sashayed across the cafeteria and deftly whispered _____ to Edward that no human could hear.
   A. a pyre
   B. an aside
   C. a cascade
   D. a catalyst
   E. a ramification

8. Smoke from the funeral _____ rose high into the sky.
   A. cataract
   B. horde
   C. mongrel
   D. pyre
   E. crypt

1. **C.** *Lithe* and *lissome* mean *graceful*. *Clamorous, obstreperous, raucous,* and *vociferous* mean *loud and harsh, especially relating to a crowd.*

2. **A.** *Grating* and *rasping* describe *a loud and harsh noise. Aloof, insouciant, cavalier,* and *perfunctory* mean *casual.*

3. **E.** *Offhand* and *dismissive* mean *casual and rude. Sentient* means *feeling,* and *agile, deft,* and *nimble* mean *graceful.*

4. **A.** *Blasé* and *apathetic* mean *bored. Limber, lissome,* and *dexterous* mean *graceful,* and *maladroit* means *clumsy.*

5. **B.** "Sashay is a confident walk."
   A. Strut is a fast walk . . . no.
   (B.) Amble is a leisurely walk . . . yes!
   C. Jog is a slow walk . . . no.
   D. Walk is an obstreperous walk (loud and harsh) . . . no.
   E. Offhand (casual) is a tense walk . . . no.

6. **A.** "Blasé (casual, bored) is the opposite of circumspect (wary)."
   (A.) Vociferous (loud and harsh) is the opposite of placid (peaceful) . . . maybe.
   B. Lithe (graceful) is the opposite of dexterous (graceful) . . . no.
   C. Haggard (exhausted) is the opposite of belligerent (hostile) . . . no.
   D. Torrent (flood) is the opposite of inundation (flood) . . . no.
   E. Incredulous (doubtful) is the opposite of dubious (doubtful) . . . no.
   Choice A is best.

7. **B.** "Alice lithely sashayed across the cafeteria and deftly whispered <u>a whisper</u> to Edward that no human could hear."
   An aside means *a whispered remark.* She may have whispered about a *ramification* (consequence) of something, but you have evidence only that she whispered and that no human could hear it.

8. **D.** "Smoke from the funeral <u>fire</u> rose high into the sky."
   Pyre means *fire, often used at a funeral* and fits best. *Crypt* means *tomb* and may have to do with funerals, but does not fit the evidence "smoke . . . rose high into the sky" as well as *pyre* does.

Group 38
Baleful Contingent

Find each of the following words on the *Eclipse* page number provided. Based on the way each word is used in the book, guess at its definition.

1. **Studiously** (p. 559) might mean _____

_____

2. **Contingent** (p. 563) might mean _____

_____

3. **Feral** (p. 571) might mean _____

_____

4. **Apathy** (p. 571) might mean _____

_____

5. **Cowl** (p. 571) might mean _____

_____

6. **Animated** (p. 572) might mean _____

_____

7. **Baleful** (p. 574) might mean _____

_____

8. **Inflectionless** (p. 574) might mean _____

_____

Let's see how you did. Check your answers, write the exact definitions, and reread the sentence in *Eclipse* where each word appears. Then complete the drills on the next page.

Definitions

1. **Studiously** (p. 559) means *deliberately* or *attentively.* That's easy to remember since it sounds so much like *studying.* Standardized tests love the synonyms *assiduously, diligently, fastidiously, meticulously, punctiliously, scrupulously,* and *sedulously.*

2. **Contingent** (p. 563) means *group.* Synonym: cohort.

3. **Feral** (p. 571) means *wild or ferocious.*

4. **Apathy** (p. 571) means *lack of feeling. Apathetically* was a synonym for *impassively* in Group 35. *Apathy* is a great word to break apart. *A-* means *not,* and *path-* refers to *feeling,* so *apathy* means *not feeling.* Synonyms: dispassion, indifference. Another super-fancy synonym is *ennui,* which is actually the French word for *boredom.*

5. **Cowl** (p. 571) means *large hood.* The *Twilight* movies often show Jane and other members of the Volturi guard wearing a cloak and cowl.

6. **Animated** (p. 572) means *lively* and was a synonym for *flamboyant* in Group 9. Animated characters are usually more **lively** than real people, though Homer Simpson and Gollum may be exceptions to that rule. Presumably, Renesme will be animated in the *Breaking Dawn* movie—she is definitely more **lively** than a typical infant!

7. **Baleful** (p. 574) means *hostile* or *evil.* Synonyms: acrimonious, maleficent, malevolent, malicious, malignant, noxious, pernicious, venomous, vindictive, vitriolic.

8. **Inflectionless** (p. 574) means *flat—without inflection* (*inflection* means *change in pitch*). Synonym: monotone.

Synonyms: Select the word or phrase whose meaning is closest to the word in capital letters.

1. STUDIOUSLY
   A. dispassionately
   B. indifferently
   C. acrimoniously
   D. malevolently
   E. sedulously

2. CONTINGENT
   A. cowl
   B. cohort
   C. pyre
   D. aside
   E. fissure

3. APATHY
   A. inflection
   B. chasm
   C. cleft
   D. ennui
   E. rift

4. BALEFUL
   A. monotone
   B. animated
   C. pernicious
   D. lithe
   E. deft

Analogies: Select the answer choice that best completes the meaning of the sentence.

5. Inflectionless is to animated as
   A. monotone is to noxious
   B. flat is to vitriolic
   C. intransigent is to punctilious
   D. assiduous is to lithe
   E. sedulous is to hasty

6. Baleful is to malicious as
   A. assiduous is to punctilious
   B. feral is to flamboyant
   C. malignant is to maladroit
   D. supple is to jaded
   E. surfeited is to strident

Sentence Completions: Choose the word that, when inserted in the sentence, *best* fits the meaning of the sentence as a whole.

7. Darlena was known for _____ proofreading; classmates often asked her to check their essays before handing them in.
   A. apathetic
   B. venomous
   C. obstreperous
   D. sedulous
   E. feral

8. Mr. Kendrick's _____ voice lulled students to sleep even during lectures on seemingly interesting subjects.
   A. soprano
   B. animated
   C. grating
   D. shrill
   E. monotone

1. **E.** *Studiously* and *sedulously* mean *attentively. Dispassionately* and *indifferently* mean *casually. Acrimoniously* and *malevolently* mean *with hostility.*

2. **B.** *Contingent* and *cohort* mean *group. Cowl* means *hood, pyre* means *funeral fire, aside* means *whispered comment,* and *fissure* means *crack.*

3. **D.** *Apathy* and *ennui* mean *lack of feeling or caring. Inflection* means *change in pitch,* and *chasm, cleft,* and *rift* mean *crack.*

4. **C.** *Baleful* and *pernicious* mean *hostile* or *evil. Monotone* means *without inflection, animated* means *lively,* and *lithe* and *deft* mean *graceful.*

5. **E.** "Inflectionless (flat) is the opposite of animated (lively)."
    A. Monotone (flat) is the opposite of noxious (hostile) . . . no.
    B. Flat is the opposite of vitriolic (hostile) . . . no.
    C. Intransigent (stubborn) is the opposite of punctilious (diligent) . . . no.
    D. Assiduous (diligent) is the opposite of lithe (graceful) . . . no.
    E. Sedulous (diligent) is the opposite of hasty (rushed) . . . yes!

6. **A.** "Baleful (hostile) means the same as malicious (hostile)."
    A. Assiduous (diligent) means the same as punctilious (diligent) . . . yes.
    B. Feral (wild) means the same as flamboyant (showy) . . . no.
    C. Malignant (evil) means the same as maladroit (clumsy) . . . no.
    D. Supple (flexible) means the same as jaded (bored) . . . no.
    E. Surfeited (bored) means the same as strident (loud and harsh) . . . no.

7. **D.** "Darlena was known for <u>excellent</u> proofreading; classmates often asked her to check their essays before handing them in."
    Sedulous means *careful.*

8. **E.** "Mr. Kendrick's <u>lulling</u> voice lulled students to sleep even during lectures on seemingly interesting subjects."
    Monotone means *flat* and is the best choice.

Group 39

Cherubic Jane?

Find each of the following words on the *Eclipse* page number provided.
Based on the way each word is used in the book, guess at its definition.

1. **Beatific** (p. 576) might mean _____

   _____

2. **Cherubic** (p. 578) might mean _____

   _____

3. **Corroborated** (p. 581) might mean _____

   _____

4. **Meticulously** (p. 581) might mean _____

   _____

5. **Monotone** (p. 583) might mean _____

   _____

6. **Empathize** (p. 585) might mean _____

   _____

7. **Sympathize** (p. 585) might mean _____

   _____

8. **Vocabulary** (p. 586) might mean _____

   _____

Let's see how you did. Check your answers, write the exact definitions, and reread the sentence in *Eclipse* where each word appears. Then complete the drills on the next page.

Definitions

1. **Beatific** (p. 576) looks like *beautiful,* but means *blissful.* People look **beautiful** when they are beaming and **blissful,** like Bella will look as a bride. That's the connection and why beatific looks so much like *beautiful.* Synonyms: ecstatic, rapturous.

2. **Cherubic** (p. 578) means *angelic.* Synonym: seraphic. Jane's appearance is, of course, deceiving; she looks like an angel, but she's **definitely** no angel.

3. **Corroborated** (p. 581) means *confirmed* or *backed up. Cor-* means *together,* and *corroborated* means *confirmed together.*

4. **Meticulously** (p. 581) means *diligently* and was a synonym for *studiously* in Group 38. For all of you who are planning to become Cullens or have added the name "Cullen" to your Facebook profile, Alice is giving you part of the family code here! Synonyms: assiduously, conscientiously, fastidiously, punctiliously, scrupulously, sedulously. Standardized tests love these words; learn them and you'll gain points!

5. **Monotone** (p. 583) means *flat, without a change in pitch.* You learned this word in Group 38 as a synonym for *inflectionless.* Bella hints at the meaning of the word *monotone* right in the sentence, "My voice was monotone, dead."

6. **Empathize** (p. 585) means *share or experience the feeling of another. Em-* means *in-,* and *path-* means *feeling,* so *empathize* means *be **in** the **feeling** with someone.*

7. **Sympathize** (p. 585) means *feel compassion for.* Alice can **sympathize** (feel compassion) for Bella, but she can't **empathize** (feel her pain). Also remember from Group 38 that *apathetic* means *lack of feeling,* since *a-* means *without* and *path-* means *feeling.* What's your feeling regarding Bella's situation: empathetic, sympathetic, or apathetic?

8. **Vocabulary** (p. 586), of course, means *list of words used.* Charlie says about Jacob, "I don't know where he picked up that vocabulary . . . ." If someone asks you that question you can say, "Where did I pick up my vocabulary? From using *Defining Eclipse,* of course!" Synonyms: lexicon, lexis.

Synonyms: Select the word or phrase whose meaning is closest to the word in capital letters.

1. BEATIFIC
   - A. assiduous
   - B. rapturous
   - C. fastidious
   - D. scrupulous
   - E. sedulous

2. CHERUBIC
   - A. monotone
   - B. empathetic
   - C. sympathetic
   - D. apathetic
   - E. seraphic

3. CORROBORATE
   - A. conspire
   - B. sashay
   - C. confirm
   - D. differentiate
   - E. discriminate

4. METICULOUS
   - A. acrimonious
   - B. maleficent
   - C. fastidious
   - D. malicious
   - E. pernicious

Analogies: Select the answer choice that best completes the meaning of the sentence.

5. Lexicon is to words as
   - A. accord is to mania
   - B. dissonance is to harmony
   - C. cornucopia is to goods
   - D. choreography is to pacifists
   - E. lattice is to prosperity

6. Beatific is to ecstatic as
   - A. cherubic is to defiant
   - B. meticulous is to urbane
   - C. monotone is to ameliorated
   - D. acute is to severe
   - E. glacial is to qualified

Sentence Completions: Choose the word that, when inserted in the sentence, *best* fits the meaning of the sentence as a whole.

7. Vaughn's study finally _____ Sheldon's controversial findings about ape habitat in the eastern Congo, proving that Sheldon had been right all along.
   - A. corroborated
   - B. defied
   - C. subverted
   - D. exploited
   - E. goaded

8. Dr. Chen required _____ attention to detail from all his interns and would overlook no slip-ups.
   - A. apathetic
   - B. beatific
   - C. assiduous
   - D. malignant
   - E. sentient

1. **B.** *Beatific* and *rapturous* mean *blissful. Assiduous, fastidious, scrupulous,* and *sedulous* mean *diligent and attentive.*

2. **E.** *Cherubic* and *seraphic* mean *angelic. Monotone* means *flat, empathetic* means *feeling with someone, sympathetic* means *feeling for someone,* and *apathetic* means *not feeling.*

3. **C.** *Corroborate* means *confirm. Conspire* means *plot, sashay* means *walk leisurely and confidently,* and *differentiate* and *discriminate* mean *tell the difference between.*

4. **C.** *Meticulous* and *fastidious* mean *attentive to detail. Acrimonious, maleficent, malicious,* and *pernicious* mean *hostile and evil.*

5. **C.** "Lexicon (words of a language) is a lot of words."
   A. Accord (treaty) is a lot of mania (madness) . . . no.
   B. Dissonance (disharmony) is a lot of harmony . . . no.
   C. Cornucopia (abundance) is a lot of goods . . . maybe.
   D. Choreography (planning) is a lot of pacifists (people who want peace) . . . no.
   E. Lattice (grid) is a lot of prosperity (abundance) . . . no.
   Using the process of elimination, choice C is best.

6. **D.** "Beatific means ecstatic (thrilled)."
   A. Cherubic (angelic) means defiant . . . no.
   B. Meticulous (diligent) means urbane (polished) . . . no.
   C. Monotone (flat) means ameliorated (soothed) . . . no.
   D. Acute (severe) means severe . . . yes!
   E. Glacial (icy) means qualified (conditional) . . . no.

7. **A.** "Vaughn's study finally <u>proved</u> Sheldon's controversial findings about ape habitat in the eastern Congo, proving that Sheldon had been right all along."
   Corroborated means *confirmed* and fits best. Vaughn may have *exploited* (made use of) Sheldon's findings, but you have evidence only that Vaughn **proved** them.

8. **C.** "Dr. Chen required <u>lots of</u> attention to detail from all his interns and would overlook no slip-ups."
   Assiduous means *diligent.*

Group 40
Obstinate Eclipse

Find each of the following words on the *Eclipse* page number provided. Based on the way each word is used in the book, guess at its definition.

1. **Gaunt** (p. 591) might mean _____

_____

2. **Eclipse** (p. 600) might mean _____

_____

3. **Adjustments** (p. 609) might mean _____

_____

4. **Disorientation** (p. 609) might mean _____

_____

5. **Annihilated** (p. 611) might mean _____

_____

6. **Obstinacy** (p. 617) might mean _____

_____

7. **Wistful** (p. 620) might mean _____

_____

8. **Eternity** (p. 620) might mean _____

_____

166 Let's see how you did. Check your answers, write the exact definitions, and reread the sentence in *Eclipse* where each word appears. Then complete the drills on the next page.

Definitions

1. **Gaunt** (p. 591) means *haggard and thin.* You learned in Group 26 that *haggard* means *exhausted and unhealthy looking.* So *gaunt* means that plus *thin* or *underfed. Gaunt* is the opposite of *animated* (lively).

2. **Eclipse** (p. 600) means *when one thing blocks the light of another,* like the moon **eclipsing** the sun, or Edward **eclipsing** Jacob to Bella. This is such a *bittersweet* (happy mixed with sad) part of the book.

3. **Adjustments** (p. 609) means *changes to make better.* This word comes from *ad-* meaning *to,* and *juxt-* meaning *near,* so *adjustments* are *changes to make something **nearer to** the way you want it. Juxt-* can also help you remember the great SAT and ACT word *juxtaposition* (**positioning** one thing **near** another to compare them).

4. **Disorientation** (p. 609) means *confusion. Dis-* means *reversal* and *orientation* means *positioning,* so *disorientation* means *reversing positioning and becoming **confused.***

5. **Annihilated** (p. 611) means *destroyed.* Synonym: obliterated.

6. **Obstinacy** (p. 617) means *stubbornness. Obstinate* was a synonym for *defiant* in Group 34. Synonyms for *obstinate:* implacable, intractable, intransigent, obdurate, pertinacious, recalcitrant, refractory, tenacious.

7. **Wistful** (p. 620) means *nostalgic or regretful longing.*

8. **Eternity** (p. 620) means *forever,* and that's the perfect word with which to end this Bella and Edward vocabulary list.

Synonyms: Select the word or phrase whose meaning is closest to the
word in capital letters.

1. GAUNT
    A. haggard
    B. eclipsed
    C. adjusted
    D. juxtaposed
    E. implacable

2. ANNIHILATED
    A. intractable
    B. intransigent
    C. obdurate
    D. pertinacious
    E. obliterated

3. OBSTINATE
    A. beatific
    B. recalcitrant
    C. corroborated
    D. assiduous
    E. sedulous

4. WISTFUL
    A. cherubic
    B. fastidious
    C. nostalgic
    D. dispassionate
    E. apathetic

Analogies: Select the answer choice that best completes the meaning
of the sentence.

5. Gaunt is to animated as
    A. annihilated is to
       obliterated
    B. refractory is to tenacious
    C. eternal is to ephemeral
    D. baleful is to pernicious
    E. venomous is to
       vindictive

6. Intractable is to obdurate as
    A. lithe is to obstreperous
    B. offhand is to sentient
    C. nimble is to maladroit
    D. vociferous is to
       clamorous
    E. tangible is to ferocious

Sentence Completions: Choose the word that, when inserted in the
sentence, *best* fits the meaning of the sentence as a whole.

7. Matthew made _____
   to the plan, hoping that
   these slight changes would
   improve his results.
    A. disorientations
    B. fissures
    C. convulsions
    D. wheedlings
    E. adjustments

8. Bella obstinately knew that
   she would love Edward
   through all _____ and
   was wistful for the many
   eons that they would share.
    A. obliteration
    B. eclipses
    C. enigmas
    D. belligerence
    E. eternity

Solutions

1. **A.** *Gaunt* means *haggard (exhausted-looking) and thin*, so *haggard* is the best choice. *Eclipsed* means *covered, adjusted* means *changed, juxtaposed* means *placed nearby for comparison,* and *implacable* means *stubborn and unsatisfiable.*

2. **E.** *Annihilated* and *obliterated* mean *destroyed. Intractable, intransigent, obdurate,* and *pertinacious* mean *stubborn.*

3. **B.** *Obstinate* and *recalcitrant* mean *stubborn. Beatific* means *blissful, corroborated* means *confirmed,* and *assiduous* and *sedulous* mean *diligent.*

4. **C.** *Wistful* means *nostalgic. Cherubic* means *angelic, fastidious* means *diligent,* and *dispassionate* and *apathetic* mean *without emotion.*

5. **C.** "Gaunt (haggard and thin) is the opposite of animated (lively)."

   A. Annihilated (destroyed) is the opposite of obliterated (destroyed) . . . no.

   B. Refractory (stubborn) is the opposite of tenacious (stubborn) . . . no.

   (C.) Eternal (forever) is the opposite of ephemeral (temporary) . . . yes!

   D. Baleful (hostile) is the opposite of pernicious (hostile) . . . no.

   E. Venomous (hostile) is the opposite of vindictive (hostile) . . . no.

6. **D.** "Intractable (stubborn) means obdurate (stubborn)."

   A. Lithe (graceful) means obstreperous (loud and unruly) . . . no.

   B. Offhand (casual) means sentient (feeling) . . . no.

   C. Nimble (graceful) means maladroit (clumsy) . . . no.

   (D.) Vociferous (loud and harsh) means clamorous (loud and harsh) . . . yes.

   E. Tangible (touchable) means ferocious (fierce) . . . no.

7. **E.** "Matthew made _changes_ to the plan, hoping that these slight changes would improve his results."

   Adjustments means *changes to make better.*

8. **E.** "Bella obstinately knew that she would love Edward through all _????_ and was wistful for the many eons that they would share."

   Eternity means *forever* and fits best.

Quiz 8

I. Let's review some of the words that you've seen in Groups 36–40. Match each of the following words to the correct definition or synonym on the right. Then check the solutions on page 172.

1. Tangible		A. Rasping
2. Fissure		B. Insouciant
3. Strident		C. Malevolent
4. Lithe		D. Surfeited
5. Offhand		E. Tactile
6. Blasé		F. Chasm
7. Contingent		G. Confirm
8. Animated		H. Deft
9. Baleful		I. Intransigent
10. Beatific		J. Blissful
11. Corroborate		K. Cohort
12. Meticulous		L. Nostalgic
13. Gaunt		M. Flamboyant
14. Obstinate		N. Haggard
15. Wistful		O. Assiduous

II. Let's review several of the word parts that you've seen in Groups 36–40. Match each of the following word parts to the correct definition or synonym on the right. Then check the solutions on page 172.

16. Sent-		A. Together
17. A-		B. Feel
18. Cor-		C. Near
19. Em-		D. In
20. Juxt-		E. Reversal
21. Dis-		F. Not

Review

Match each group of synonyms to its general meaning. Then check the solutions on page 172.

1. Circumspect
   Vigilant
   Wary

   A. Varied

2. Ephemeral
   Evanescent
   Fleeting
   Impermanent
   Transient
   Transitory

   B. Inborn

3. Diverse
   Heterogeneous
   Manifold
   Motley
   Multifarious
   Sundry
   Variegated

   C. Watchful

4. Gooey
   Inherent
   Innate
   Intrinsic

   D. Overly sentimental

5. Cloying
   Mawkish
   Saccharine
   Treacly

   E. Diligent

6. Assiduous
   Fastidious
   Meticulous
   Punctilious
   Scrupulous
   Sedulous

   F. Temporary

Quiz and Review Solutions

Quiz 1	Quiz 2	Quiz 3	Quiz 4	Groups 1-20 Review
1. D	1. D	1. D	1. C	1. C
2. A	2. F	2. F	2. E	2. F
3. E	3. A	3. A	3. A	3. G
4. B or M	4. B	4. B	4. B	4. B
5. H	5. H	5. H	5. I	5. A
6. C	6. C	6. C	6. D	6. D
7. J	7. K	7. J	7. J	7. E
8. I	8. E	8. E	8. K	
9. B or M	9. I	9. M	9. L	
10. F	10. O	10. O	10. F	
11. O	11. N	11. N	11. G	
12. N	12. G	12. G	12. O	
13. G	13. M	13. I	13. N	
14. L	14. J	14. L	14. H	
15. K	15. L	15. K	15. M	
16. E	16. E	16. C	16. C	
17. D	17. A	17. A	17. D	
18. B	18. F	18. F	18. F	
19. A	19. B	19. B	19. B	
20. C or F	20. C	20. D	20. A	
21. C or F	21. D	21. E	21. E	

Answers to:

Group 18 question: Dr. Preston Burke said this to Dr. Cristina Yang. (ABC, *Grey's Anatomy*, "Yesterday," 2006.)

Group 19 question: Blair Waldorf said this to Serena about her annual sleepover. (The CW, *Gossip Girl*, "Dare Devil," 2007)

Quiz 5	Quiz 6	Quiz 7	Quiz 8	Groups 21–40 Review
1. E	1. E	1. C	1. E	1. C
2. F	2. A	2. G	2. F	2. F
3. A	3. C	3. A	3. A	3. A
4. G	4. G	4. F	4. H	4. B
5. B	5. B	5. H	5. B	5. D
6. K	6. I	6. B	6. D	6. E
7. N	7. D	7. K	7. K	
8. O	8. F	8. D	8. M	
9. C	9. M	9. I	9. C	
10. D	10. N	10. E	10. J	
11. M	11. O	11. O	11. G	
12. H	12. H	12. N	12. O	
13. I	13. J	13. L	13. N	
14. L	14. L	14. J	14. I	
15. J	15. K	15. M	15. L	
16. D	16. D	16. D	16. B	
17. A	17. A	17. F	17. F	
18. F	18. E	18. B	18. A	
19. E	19. C or F	19. E	19. D	
20. B	20. C or F	20. A	20. C	
21. C	21. B	21. C	21. E	

Glossary

Abashed embarrassed

Abstract theoretical rather than actual

Abstraction distracted thinking. Synonym: *woolgathering*

Accelerant something that accelerates (speeds up) the spread of fire. Synonym: *catalyst*

Acute severe or sharp

Adjustments changes to make better

Adulation extreme admiration. Synonym: *veneration*

Alibi excuse. Synonym: *pretext*

Alleviate relieve. Synonyms: *abate, allay, ameliorate, assuage, conciliate, mitigate, mollify, pacify, placate, propitiate, temper*

Alpha the first letter of the Greek alphabet or the one in the first position—the one in charge

Ambled walked in a leisurely way

Ambulate walk

Ambulatory mobile, able to walk, related to walking

Amenable willing or open to an idea. Synonyms: *acquiescent, compliant, obliging*

Analogy comparison

Anguish suffering

Animated lively

Annihilated destroyed. Synonym: *obliterated*

Anonymity not being identified

Anticlimactic disappointing. Synonym: *bathetic*

Antiquity the ancient past

Apathy lack of feeling. Synonyms: *dispassion, ennui, indifference*

Appalled horrified

Appease satisfy. Synonyms: *ameliorate, assuage, conciliate, mollify, pacify, placate, propitiate*

Aside whispered remark

Aspirations desires

Avalanche massive sliding of ice, rock, or snow

Avid eager or enthusiastic. Synonyms: *ardent, keen, zealous*

Baleful hostile or evil. Synonyms: *acrimonious, maleficent, malevolent, malicious, malignant, noxious, pernicious, venomous, vindictive, vitriolic*

Banal overused and boring. Synonyms: *cliché, hackneyed, hokey, platitudinous, trite*

Barren empty, bleak, or lifeless. Synonyms: *desolate, disconsolate*

Beatific blissful. Synonyms: *ecstatic, rapturous*

Beleaguered troubled or attacked. Synonym: *besieged*

Bellicose warlike

Belligerent hostile

Berserk crazy, out of control

Beseeching begging. Synonyms: *entreating, imploring, importuning*

Beta the second letter of the Greek alphabet or the one in the second position

Blasé bored and nonchalant. Synonyms: *jaded, surfeited*

Bleak gloomy, not hopeful

Boisterously with excitement

Bowery like a bower (a shady place). Synonyms for bower: *alcove, arbor, gazebo, grotto, pergola, sanctuary*

Bravado boldness meant to hide something or impress. Synonyms: *bluster, boasting, bombast, braggadocio, bragging, machismo, swaggering*

Brusquely abruptly or rudely. Synonyms: *curtly, gruffly, offhandedly, tersely*

Capitalize on make use of. Synonym: *exploit*

Carnage killing

Catalyst motivator. Synonyms: *impetus, precipitant, stimulus*

Catatonic unresponsive and in a stupor

Chagrin annoyance and embarrassment

Cherubic angelic. Synonym: *seraphic*

Choreography arrangement of dancers

Cipher code

Circumspectly carefully. Synonyms: *vigilant, wary*

Civilized well-mannered. Synonyms: *polished, urbane*

Clandestine secret, especially for something immoral. Synonyms: *covert, furtive, on the sly, surreptitious*

Clerical pertaining to a religious minister; or relating to office work. Synonym: *sacerdotal*

Coaxing persuading in a gentle way. Synonyms for coax: *cajole, enjoin, entreat, exhort, goad, implore, incite, inveigle, prod, spur*

Coercion actions that persuade someone to do something. Synonym: *duress*

Coexisting existing together peacefully

Commemorate honor and celebrate

Companionable relaxed and friendly. Synonyms: *affable, amiable, convivial, cordial, genial, gregarious*

Compiled gathered

Complacently smugly

Complement amount. Synonym: *contingent*

Comrades companions

Concealment hiding

Condescendingly with a superior attitude. Synonyms: *haughty, patronizing, supercilious*

Conditionally with a condition or reservation. Synonyms for conditional: *mitigated, qualified, tempered*

Conflagrations fires

Congealed thickened and grouped

Conjoined joined together

Connotations implications

Connubial related to marriage

Consensus agreement. Synonyms: *accord, concurrence*

Conspires plots

Consternation distress at something unexpected

Contingent group. Synonym: *cohort*

Convivial lively

Convulsion spasm

Cornucopia abundance. Synonyms: *profusion, surfeit*

Correspondence communication at a distance

Corroborated confirmed or backed up

Coveted wanted

Cowl large hood

Crimson purplish-red

Crux main point or essence

Crypt tomb. Synonyms: *ossuary, sepulcher*

Custodial relating to protective or parental care

Decipherable understandable

Defiant defying, resisting, or challenging. Synonyms: *dissenting, insubordinate, intransigent, noncompliant, obstinate, obstreperous, recalcitrant, subversive, truculent (very defiant)*

Demise destruction or death

Deprecatingly in a belittling or criticizing way. Synonyms: *denigratingly, disparagingly, pejoratively*

Derail knock off the track

Deranged crazed. Synonyms: *berserk, frenzied, insane, irrational, unbalanced, unhinged, unstable*

Derogatory critical. Synonyms: *defamatory, denigrating, depreciatory, disparaging, pejorative*

Desperation distress and lack of hope

Dexterous graceful and skilled. Synonyms: *adept, adroit, agile, deft, nimble*

Diction one's style of speaking or writing

Dictum proclamation

Differentiate tell the difference between. Synonyms: *discriminate, distinguish*

Diffused spread out

Dirge expression of mourning, like a song or poem at a funeral. Synonyms: *elegy, lament, requiem, threnody*

Discord disagreement or disharmony. Synonym: *dissonance*

Disorientation confusion

Dissension disagreement

Distended swollen

Diverse varied. Synonyms: *heterogeneous, manifold, motley, multifarious, sundry, variegated*

Diverted distracted

Divine Godlike, noble and admirable

Duress actions that forcibly persuade someone to do something. Synonym: *coercion*

Dutifully fulfilling a duty or obligation

Eclipse when one thing blocks the light of another

Ecstatic thrilled. Synonyms: *buoyant, ebullient, elated, euphoric, exuberant, exultant, jubilant, rapturous*

Elimination removal, killing

Empathize share or experience the feeling of another

Encroach intrude on. Synonym: *obtrude*

Engendered created

Enigmatic mysterious or difficult to understand and interpret. Synonyms: *abstruse, arcane, impenetrable, inscrutable, recondite*

Enormity hugeness or importance, enormousness

Epidemic outbreak

Epiphany sudden insight

Epoch period of history. Synonyms: *eon, era*

Era a period of time in history. Synonyms: *eon, epoch*

Errant stray

Escalation increase or bring things to the next level. Synonyms: *amplification, augmentation, exacerbation (increase and make worse)*

Essence fundamental nature. Synonyms: *crux, quintessence*

Eternity forever

Euphoric thrilled. Synonyms: *buoyant, ebullient, ecstatic, elated, euphoric, exultant, jubilant, rapturous*

Evasively avoidingly

Exacerbated increased and made worse

Exasperated very frustrated

Extricated freed. Synonym: *disentangled*

Exuberance excitement. Synonyms for exuberant: *buoyant, ebullient, ecstatic, elated, euphoric, exultant, jubilant, rapturous*

Exuding giving off or radiating

Exultant thrilled. Synonyms: *ebullient, ecstatic, elated, euphoric, exuberant, jubilant, rapturous*

Exultation happiness and triumph

Farce sham or lie. Synonyms: *charade, pretense*

Federal national, as opposed to state

Feigning pretending

Feinting faking a movement. Synonyms for feint: *artifice, chicanery, contrivance, duplicity, guile, hoax, pretense, ruse, subterfuge*

Feline catlike

Feral wild or ferocious

Ferocious fierce and violent. Synonyms: *merciless, ruthless, savage*

Fervor passion. Synonyms: *ardor, zeal*

Fiancé man engaged to be married. Synonym: *betrothed*

Fiancée woman engaged to be married. Synonym: *betrothed*

Fissure crack. Synonyms: *breach, chasm, cleft, crevasse, crevice, fault, fracture, rift, rupture*

Flamboyant showy, standing out. Synonyms: *animated, exuberant*

Forlorn miserable or hopeless

Fortnight two-week period

Fretting worrying

Gangly tall, skinny, and awkward. Synonym: *lanky*

Gaunt haggard and thin

Generic common, not special, or nonspecific

Genetic relating to genes or heredity

Genocide killing of a racial group

Glacial cold or unfriendly

Glacier massive, slow-moving river of ice

Glutton a person greedy or overeager for something

Gooey sticky or emotionally sappy. Synonyms: *cloying, mawkish, saccharine, sentimental, treacly*

Grandiose very grand or extravagant

Grating loud and harsh Synonyms: *clamorous, obstreperous, rasping, raucous, shrill, strident, vociferous*

Gregarious friendly, social

Hackles hairs on the back of a dog (or wolf) or person's head that straighten when the animal or person is angry or frightened

Haggard looking exhausted and unwell

Havoc disorder or destruction. Synonyms: *anarchy, bedlam, mayhem, pandemonium, rumpus, tumult, turmoil*

Hefty large, heavy, and powerful

Heinous wicked

Hemorrhage burst of blood

Herculean requiring tremendous strength. Synonym: *arduous*

Hokey corny, overused, or overly sentimental. Synonyms: *banal (overused and boring), cliché, hackneyed, platitudinous, trite*

Homicides murders

Horde mob

Hyperbole exaggeration

Impassively without emotion. Synonyms: *apathetically, dispassionately, indifferently*

Impending looming or coming soon. Synonyms: *forthcoming, imminent*

Implacable unable to be satisfied or unstoppable. Synonyms: *inexorable, intransigent, relentless, unappeasable*

Import extra significance

Imprinting making an impression

Impromptu spontaneous

Incorrigible unapologetic and unlikely to change. Synonyms: *impenitent, inveterate, irredeemable, remorseless*

Incredulous unbelieving. Synonym: *dubious*

Indisputable not disputable—definite

Indulgent overly generous. Synonyms: *forbearing, lenient, liberal, permissive*

Inept clumsy and unskilled. Synonym: *maladroit*

Inert inactive

Inevitability unavoidability. Synonym: *inexorableness*

Infestation overabundance of animals or insects

Inflectionless flat, without inflection (change in tone). Synonym: *monotone*

Injunction formal order. Synonyms: *decree, dictum, directive, edict, fiat, mandate, proclamation, writ*

Innate inborn. Synonyms: *inherent, intrinsic*

Insatiable unquenchable. Synonyms: *gluttonous, ravenous, unappeasable, voracious, wolfish*

Interceded stepped in or intervened

Interjected interrupted

Interlocution a dialogue or conversation **between** people

In vain useless. Synonym: *futile*

Ire anger. Synonyms: *fury, wrath*

Ironclad definite

Jibes joking jabs, agreement, or a sailing maneuver. Synonyms: *jeers, taunts*

Judiciously wisely. Synonyms of judicious: *astute, perspicacious, sagacious, shrewd*

Juvenile childish or immature. Synonyms: *puerile, sophomoric*

Juxtaposition positioning one thing near another to compare them

Laboriously with much hard labor. Synonym for laborious: *arduous*

Lament expression of sorrow. Synonyms: *dirge, elegy, requiem, threnody*

Lattice interwoven grid. Synonyms: *fretwork, grille, network, trellis*

Lavish extravagant and luxurious. Synonyms: *opulent, sumptuous*

Lee sheltered from weather

Libertine free thinker

Liberty freedom

Lineage ancestors

Lithely gracefully. Synonyms for lithe: *agile, deft, limber, lissome, lithesome, nimble, supple, willowy*

Loathing hatred. Synonyms: *abhorrence, abomination, animosity, animus, antipathy, detestation, enmity, execration, malice, odium*

Loophole hole in the rules

Loquacious talkative

Ludicrous unreasonable or ridiculous

Macabre gruesome. Synonyms: *ghastly, gory, grotesque, grisly, hideous, morbid*

Majesty dignity

Maladroit unskilled, clumsy

Malignant evil, infectious, or cancerous. Synonyms: *maleficent, malevolent, malicious, vengeful, vindictive*

Mania madness or obsession

Marred damaged or spoiled

Matrimony marriage

Medusa Greek mythological female monster who had snakes for hair

Metaphor when two things are compared **without** using the words **like** or **as**

Meticulously diligently. Synonyms: *assiduously, conscientiously, fastidiously, punctiliously, scrupulously, sedulously, studiously*

Modus operandi way of doing something. Synonym: *methodology*

Mollified soothed. Synonyms: *abate, allay, alleviate, ameliorate, appease, assuage, conciliate, mitigate, pacify, placate, propitiate, temper*

Mongrel mix of breeds. Synonym: *mutt*

Monotone flat, without a change in pitch. Synonym: *inflectionless*

Morosely gloomily

Multitudinous many

Musk ingredient in colognes that comes from a secretion of the male musk deer

Musky outdoorsy, masculine scent

Mutually exclusive unable to occur at the same time

Nadir lowest point

Nautical pertaining to sailing

Neophyte person who is new to something—a newbie. Synonyms: *novice, novitiate, postulant, tenderfoot, tyro*

Nomads wanderers. Synonyms: *itinerants, transients*

Objectively without being influenced by personal feelings. Synonyms of objective: *dispassionate, impartial, nonpartisan, unbiased*

Obscured hidden. Synonyms for obscure: *abstruse, recondite*

Obstinacy stubbornness. Synonyms for obstinate: *defiant, implacable, intractable, intransigent, obdurate, pertinacious, recalcitrant, refractory, tenacious*

Obtuse thick, slow to comprehend

Offhand nonchalant, often to the point of being rude. Synonyms: *aloof, blasé, cavalier, dismissive, glib, indifferent, insouciant, nonchalant, perfunctory*

Omnipresent common or present all over. Synonym: *ubiquitous*

Omniscience the state of knowing everything

On the sly secretly. Synonyms: *clandestinely, covertly, furtively, surreptitiously*

Orchestrate plan or arrange the various parts of something to produce a certain result

Organza thin, stiff fabric, usually used in formalwear

Overt obvious

Pacific peaceful

Pacifist someone who seeks peace, as opposed to violence and war

Pandemonium chaos. Synonyms: *anarchy, bedlam, mayhem, rumpus, tumult, turmoil*

Paranormal beyond normal

Parasites creatures that live off others, without giving in return

Parole release with the promise of good behavior

Paroxysms attacks, usually of an emotion or activity, such as laughter or crying

Peeved irritated. Synonym: *in high dudgeon*

Pensively thoughtfully

Percolating bubbling or spreading

Perverse deviant

Pessimist someone who imagines that bad things will happen

Petulant grumpy and irritable. Synonyms: *churlish, curmudgeonly, fractious, peevish, querulous*

Pinnacle highest point. Synonyms: *acme, apex, apogee, peak, zenith*

Placate soothe. Synonyms: *allay, alleviate, appease, assuage, conciliate, mollify, pacify*

Plaintive sad. Synonyms: *doleful, dolorous, forlorn, melancholy, mournful, pathetic, pitiful, wistful, woebegone, wretched*

Pleasantry pleasant, unimportant conversation

Plural more than one

Polarized clearly divided

Predators hunters

Prerequisite something required before

Prolific producing many works, abundant, or widespread. Synonyms: *bountiful, copious, fecund, plenteous, profuse*

Promiscuous sexually liberal

Prophecy prediction

Proportions parts of the whole

Pros and cons reasons to do or not to do something

Prosperity success

Proximity nearness. Synonym: *propinquity*

Pseudonym a false or pen name

Purge get rid of something or cleanse

Pyre heap of stuff to burn, often at a funeral

Quailed felt or showed anxiety

Ramifications negative effects

Rampage out-of-control behavior

Rebuttal denial. Synonyms: *contradiction, refutation*

Reclusive solitary

Reconcile settle

Redeeming something that makes up for something else

Reluctant hesitant

Reproach scolding. Synonyms: *admonishment, censure, rebuke, reprimand, reproof*

Reproof scolding. Synonyms: *admonishment, censure, rebuke, reprimand, reproach*

Rescinded taken back. Synonyms: *nullified, revoked*

Reservations conditions or qualifications

Ruefully regretfully

Sashayed strutted casually and confidently

Sate satisfy

Satellite something orbiting or dependent on another

Scarlet bright red

Scathingly with criticism and anger

Self-righteous with a superior attitude. Synonym: *sanctimonious*

Sentient living and feeling

Serenely peacefully or calmly

Servitude enslavement. Synonym: *subjugation (being controlled)*

Sidelong sideways and implies a secret, disguised look out of the corner of one's eyes. Synonyms: *covert, furtive, indirect, oblique, sly, surreptitious*

Simile comparison of two things using **like** or **as**

Slovenly messy

Soiree evening party

Somber serious or gloomy

Sophisticated advanced, complex, mature, or fashionable

Soprano highest singing voice

Staccato with individual, detached notes, rather than with flowing, connected notes

Stern serious or strict; also, the back of a ship

Stridently loudly and harshly. Synonyms for strident: *clamorous, grating, obstreperous, rasping, raucous, shrill, vociferous*

Stringent strict. Synonym: *stern*

Studiously deliberately or attentively. Synonyms: *assiduously, diligently, fastidiously, meticulously, punctiliously, sedulously*

Subjective influenced by personal feelings

Subterfuge trickery or deception. Synonyms: *artifice, chicanery, duplicity, guile*

Succinct brief, informative, and clear. Synonym: *compendious, concise*

Succumbed gave in

Supercilious arrogant

Superficial shallow or on the surface

Surfeited having an overabundance and becoming **bored** with it

Surly rude and unfriendly. Synonyms: *abrupt, brusque, cantankerous, churlish, curt*

Switzerland mountainous country that has remained neutral throughout several wars

Sympathize feel compassion for

Tangible touchable or real. Synonyms: *corporeal, palpable, tactile*

Tawny yellowish-brown. Synonym: *fulvous*

Tendonitis inflammation of a tendon

Tenor the highest male singing voice

Tenuous weak

Torrent outpouring or flood. Synonyms: *cascade, cataract, deluge, inundation, spate*

Touchable real and definite. Synonyms: *palpable, tangible*

Transformation change from one thing to another. Synonym: *metamorphosis*

Transient nomad, wanderer

Transitory temporary. Synonyms: *ephemeral, evanescent, fleeting, impermanent, transient*

Transmutation change

Trite overused. Synonyms: *banal (overused and boring), cliché, hackneyed, hokey, platitudinous*

Truce ceasefire. Synonyms: *armistice, entente*

Ulterior hidden or future

Ultimatum final demand, usually given as a threat

Unassailable not attackable, definite. Synonyms: *impregnable, incontrovertible, indisputable, indubitable, invincible, inviolable, invulnerable, irrefutable, manifest, patent, unconquerable*

Unchaste sexually liberal

Unfathomable impossible to understand. Synonyms: *enigmatic, impenetrable, inscrutable*

Unrepentant without regret. Synonyms: *impenitent, remorseless*

Unscrupulous stopping at nothing, immoral, or unfair. Synonyms: *conscienceless, reprobate, shameless, unethical*

Unveiled unhidden

Utilitarian useful or practical, rather than appealing. Synonym: *pragmatic*

Valedictorian highest-ranked student in the class

Vanity too much pride in one's looks. Synonym: *narcissism*

Vendetta quest for revenge

Vigilant watchful, especially for danger. Synonyms: *circumspect, wary*

Vindictive revengeful. Synonym: *vengeful*

Vocabulary list of words used. Synonyms: *lexicon, lexis*

Volatile unstable

Wane decrease

Wax increase

Wheedling using sweetness to persuade

Wistful nostalgic or regretful longing

Wrangled argued, usually about something complex; round up

Take a bite out of tedious studying
and unlock your vocabulary
potential with *Defining Twilight*

Vocabulary Workbook for Unlocking
the *SAT, ACT®, GED®, and SSAT®

defining twilight

BRIAN LEAF, M.A.
This publication has not been prepared, approved, or licensed by any
entity that created or produced the *Twilight* series of books or movies.

Join Edward and Bella as you learn more than 600 vocabulary words
to improve your score on the *SAT, ACT®, GED®, and SSAT® exams

Visit cliffsnotes.com/go/definingtwilight
Available wherever books are sold.

WILEY
Now you know.

*SAT is a registered trademark of the College Board, which was not involved in the production of, and does not endorse, this product.